# IT'S NOT ABOUT YOU

*Winning New Business in a Crowded Agency World*

by Robin & Stephen Boehler

Published by Kingbird Press
www.kingbirdpress.com



ISBN:
978-1-965629-07-9 (Paperback)
978-1-965629-08-6 (eBook)

Cover concept by Shadley Grei
Book layout and design by Timothy J. Prough

AI-assisted tools were used in the creation of this book.

## Praise for

# IT'S NOT ABOUT YOU

*Winning New Business in a Crowded Agency World*

"It's Not About You *is a gift to ad agencies trying to win new business and do better work. I highly recommend it because nobody knows this stuff better than Steve and Robin.*"

**Mark Figliulo, CEO, FIG**

*"This book captures mistakes I've seen and made myself, and it frames them in a way that's hard to forget. The lessons are simple to understand but often difficult to recognize in your own pitching, which is what makes this guide so valuable. Steve and Robin have managed thousands of pitches, and it's a gift to have their experience distilled into something the whole industry can learn from."*

**Justin Hayashi, CEO, New Engen**

*"Step inside the high-stakes world of new business pitches with Steve and Robin Boehler — trusted advisors who know exactly how brilliant agencies win and why so many others fall short. Drawing from decades at the front lines of agency/client matchmaking, Steve and Robin reveal the formulas, insider strategies, and step-by-step roadmaps that turn underdogs into champions.*

*In these pages, you'll discover proven techniques used by the most successful agencies to capture attention, master chemistry, and consistently close the deal with dream clients. Whether your shop is seasoned or just starting out, you'll learn what top brands want to see — and how to deliver it with confidence.*

*Follow the guidance in this book, and your agency could become unrecognizable — in the best way possible — a year from now. Ready to claim your seat at the winner's table? The transformation starts here."*

**Drew McLellan, CEO, Agency Management Institute**

*"Agencies always ask how to stand out in a pitch. Steve and Robin Boehler offer the clearest answer I've seen.* It's Not About You *not only explains what prospects actually value, it gives agencies practical tools to act on — from website rubrics to RFP strategies. This is the new handbook for agency business development, written by search consultants who've seen thousands of pitches."*

**Olivia Morley, Founder, FusionFront Media**

*"To kick off their book with 'It's Tough Out There' is an understatement in today's market. Mercer Island Group has always been about helping brands find partners who truly champion their goals, and their track record speaks for itself. This book feels like having their guidance at your side — helping agencies show up authentically, avoid common pitfalls, and build partnerships that last. It's an invaluable read for agency teams. Grab a highlighter!"*

**Janet Casey, Managing Partner, Gravity Global**

"It's Not About You *is outstanding work — maybe the most thorough, thoughtful, specific, and actionable agency guide I've ever seen. BRAVO. I loved it and learned a ton."*

**Marc Landsberg, CEO, Social Deviant**

*"Is there anyone more knowledgeable and insightful than Robin and Steve Boehler and the Mercer Island Group about what agencies need to do better to win more pitches? I don't think so.* It's Not About You *is a must-read guide for agencies and other professional service firms that regularly pitch their capabilities and case studies to win new clients.* It's Not About You *gets to the heart of the issues standing between agencies with great talent but average client win rates. It's packed with decades of insightful real-world success stories and user-friendly lessons that can elevate win rates and reduce the blunders we all make when we put bragging about ourselves ahead of digging into the needs of prospects. This guide is a client acquisition gold mine."*

**Brad Casper, CEO, Heart & Soul**

*"For decades, Steve and Robin have been in the room, watching thousands of agencies present and then leading client-side debriefs to decide who wins and who doesn't.*

*That invaluable lens is what makes this book indispensable. Every strategic insight comes from what they have seen work and what they have seen fail in the real world, in front of real clients, with millions of dollars of budget on the line.*

It's Not About You *is a field guide with brilliant strategy blended with specific examples and practical exercises that will transform your new business conversations into trust-building moments. If you're serious about winning more new business, your entire team needs to study this book."*

**Stephen Woessner, CEO, Predictive ROI**

*"Every agency new business professional should consider reading this book. With the experience that comes from having run hundreds of reviews, Robin and Steve have written a practical, common-sense playbook that can help*

*agencies win more business. Not only is it a recap of many things agencies probably know, but may fail to execute during a review, it also includes a number of ideas that will likely be new for many readers. Given the energy, time, and expense an agency puts into participating in a review, it makes sense to leverage every advantage you can. This book is a great guide."*

**Matt Kasindorf, American Association of Advertising Agencies**

*"Learning the Mercer Island Group method of pitching new business was new for us. The intro letter, the Five Slides, the manifesto video, the deep research, and strategy work. Some of our team initially resisted, and at one point, we had a few in tears one day because it was so hard and took so much time. But when we followed it, our very first pitch using this method landed us an 8-million-dollar account. We are believers and do our pitches this way every time."*

**Lora Kellogg, CEO, Curious Jane**

# CONTENTS

# FOREWORD

The boardroom was silent. I glanced at the screen, then at Robin. One look. No words. And I knew we were losing this pitch.

All that time.

All that money.

Gone in the first five slides.

That was my first real lesson in business development: The pitch isn't a platform for self-promotion. It's a stage for solving the prospect's problem. And the consultants in the room? They're not critics. They're your secret weapon.

Nobody has cracked the code for new business success better than Robin and Steve Boehler.

I met Robin and Steve in 2018, at the start of my BD career, and I've been learning from them ever since. To me, they've been like advertising parents — tough when they needed to be, supportive when it mattered, and always reminding me to do my homework.

I'll never forget a feedback call after a tissue session. We thought we were on track, but Robin and Steve told us the hard truth: "You need to scrap everything." Every slide. Every idea. Brutal. But we listened. We rebuilt. And we won. That moment taught me a lesson I've carried ever since: Feedback is a gift. Sometimes, it's the only thing standing between losing and winning.

Over the years, I've joined their reviews, attended their conferences, leaned on them for pitch consulting, and even brought them in for a two-day workshop with our entire company. Every time, we walked away sharper than before.

Their lessons reshaped how I think about growth. Keep your storefront prospect ready. Strategy over spec. A process that's consistent yet flexible. And above all — ask great questions. It's amazing how many agencies forget that step.

Their guidance didn't just make our phones ring and our pitches smarter. It transformed the trajectory of our agency. We've won major accounts and industry awards and built a culture where new business isn't a department — it's everyone's business.

New business is the lifeline of every agency, and this is the playbook: a collection of lessons and stories from the best in our field. Whether you're chasing your first win or sharpening your story, what's inside will make you rethink everything: your positioning, your process, your case studies, your pitch, even how you listen.

Whenever someone asks me, *"How does Curiosity do it?"* my answer is always the same: Go to Mercer Island Group conferences. Do what they teach you.

Now my answer is even easier: Read this book. Then do the work.

Ashley Walters
*Partner & CMO of Curiosity*

# INTRODUCTION
# Bruce Springsteen, Jimmy Iovine, & Winning More Pitches

It was 2013. We were proud parents sitting in the audience at the University of Southern California's commencement ceremony. The keynote speaker was Jimmy Iovine, the famous music producer and co-founder of Beats headphones. During his speech, we learned the most important lesson about new business pitching from a story Jimmy told about Bruce Springsteen. We've applied the moral to that story to sales conversations ever since.

As we remember it, Jimmy described his start as a sound engineer working on an early Bruce Springsteen album. After working on *Born to Run* with producer Jon Landau, he was asked to work on the follow-up album, *Darkness on the Edge of Town*.

Jimmy was tasked to find the right drum beat for a song, and it wasn't an easy job. After spending six weeks working around the clock trying to get the sound that Bruce had in his head actualized with instruments, Jimmy became frustrated. Bruce wanted a specific sound that he had trouble describing, and Jimmy was failing time after time to deliver what the Boss was looking for. No matter what they tried, it wasn't working. Bruce kept rejecting the work, which left Jimmy feeling disrespected and on the verge of quitting.

It was then that Bruce's manager looked Jimmy straight in the eye and said something to the effect of, "You go back there and say to Bruce, 'I'm here to support you. This is not about me. It's about the album.' You will have a friend for the rest of your life."

Jimmy swallowed his pride and did just that.

In the end, Jimmy never nailed the drumbeat.

However, six weeks later, Springsteen gave Jimmy the song "Because the Night" and asked him to produce the record for Patti Smith. Bruce was impressed with Jimmy's resolve and commitment to helping him succeed.

"Because the Night" was Jimmy's first producer gig. It went on to become a huge hit. And that experience started Jimmy on a career path towards being a billionaire.

How does this story connect to agency work, pitching for new business, and engaging with prospects?

Everything.

This is about the mindset you adopt when approaching prospects long before you step into the pitch.

It's about how you talk with prospects.

It's about how you prepare your proposal or presentation.

A winning pitch is 99% about how you think about the prospect. And your frame of mind needs to be "this is not about you."

Having sat on the client side of countless agency pitches, we've witnessed many firms fall short of this principle, and it's always a letdown. The truth is that agencies can significantly improve their success rate by shifting their mindset. As Bruce's manager wisely advised, the key is to focus on supporting the prospect, not on showcasing yourself.

It's easy to walk into a pitch and tell the client all about you. You're proud of your firm's capabilities and track record, and being invited in can feel like an invitation to share your story.

But prospects have one thing on their minds: their needs. Agencies that lead with their own accomplishments lose the room fast, while those that speak first to a prospect's challenges earn immediate attention.

To have an impactful conversation, you must understand a prospect's situation before you step into the room. That clarity requires research, preparation, and a genuine effort to grasp the problems or opportunities they're facing.

In a crowded marketplace, prospects have endless choices. The quickest way to stand out is to connect their needs to your expertise. As Jon Landau told Jimmy Iovine: **It's Not About You**. It's about the prospect and their business.

In the end, you won't nail every drumbeat or pitch, but by reframing your approach to focus first on the prospect's situation, you will dramatically increase your success rate.

Let's get to it.

# CHAPTER 1
# It's Tough Out There: Navigating a Crowded Agency Landscape

**It's tough to grow an agency.**

The U.S. is home to thousands of marketing services agencies, each vying for attention and business.

In such a crowded and fragmented field, standing out is no easy feat.

Getting a prospect's attention is tough.

It's hard to win business with that much competition.

**We're here to help.**

With over 30 years of experience studying agency-client dynamics, we've observed and participated in thousands of pitches and discussions.

We work closely every day with the client-side decision-makers who select their agencies. We're present at the meeting before the meeting and in the follow-up discussions afterward. These critical moments have provided us with invaluable insights into what works, what doesn't, and how agencies can become more prospect focused.

We wrote this book out of a deep love for agencies and a genuine passion for the marketing industry. What we've shared here has the power to help any agency thrive and succeed.

**Competition Is Greater Than Ever.**

It can be harder today than ever before to land new business. The competition is greater than it's ever been. Anyone can call themselves a marketing company, regardless of their experience or expertise. Unlike many industries or services, there are no education, certification or license requirements, and very few barriers to entry.

The competitive landscape has evolved significantly, with a growing diversity in the types of companies you're now up against. In the past, the agency world was dominated by two main categories: advertising agencies (like Ogilvy & Mather or Leo Burnett) and public relations firms (like Edelman). But that's no longer the case! Today, the field is crowded with a wide array of specialized players, including performance marketers, experiential marketing firms, CX and UX specialists, shopper agencies, social marketing firms, and SEO experts — and the list seems endless. On top of that, large consulting firms are acquiring agencies to expand their service offering, and over 80% of major corporations have launched their own in-house agencies. The competition has never been more varied — or more intense.

Agencies that tried to hold out by diversifying their capabilities have mostly become extinct. A creative agency that didn't incorporate digital is gone or has merged with a digital agency, oftentimes with the digital entity taking the lead and the creative element working in support. This has happened time and time again, with some of the most iconic agencies that built the foundation for the advertising industry. It is no surprise that when creative shop Y&R merged with digital agency VML, it became VMLY&R. Similarly, when creative shop JWT merged with Wunderman, the result was Wunderman Thompson. And more recently, all of these agencies simply became VML.

Distinctions between these different kinds of agencies are not as clear as they once were. There was a time not long ago when creative agencies didn't offer digital services, and digital agencies didn't provide traditional branding. But now, the lines are not as heavily drawn between one type of agency and another, and all different kinds of agencies are going after the same business.

For example, a potential client needs help building their social media presence. Some agencies specialize in social media. And many PR agencies can handle that scope. As can a typical ad agency, digital agency, or media consultancy. This leaves potential clients confused by both the number of options and the various services available. Clients are looking for specific types of agencies to meet their needs, and agencies are striving to offer more options to win more business.

With so many options available, prospects often feel overwhelmed and unsure of where to turn. Meanwhile, agencies are scrambling to differentiate themselves and emerge as the obvious choice. After all, every agency needs new business to thrive. But in a sea of thousands of firms offering help, how do you get your agency front and center of that consideration?

Amid all this competition, agencies often face three challenges that weaken their success rate:

1. Agencies aren't ready to be found.
2. Agencies don't know how to be found.
3. Agencies don't effectively pitch once they are found.

Agencies that know how to address each of these challenges land more new business.

## Challenge 1: Be Ready to Be Found

We've frequently heard agencies say, "If we can just get in the room, we'll prove we're the best agency for the job."

So, how do you plan to get in the room? You can't showcase your strength if you're not even invited to the party. Preparing for that opportunity means investing in your agency first. Several critical readiness steps are essential for growth — steps you overlook at your own risk.

The first step in this journey is to define your agency's positioning, making it crystal clear what kind of agency you are and why you stand out. This involves two key elements: understanding your agency's identity (your frame of reference) and articulating what makes your shop unique and appealing from a prospect's perspective.

The second step is to make sure your website is prospect-friendly, so when a prospect does discover you, they immediately see you as a potential partner. A prospect-friendly website allows visitors to find the information they're looking for quickly and effortlessly.

Of course, all of this requires time and resources — and many agencies operate on razor-thin margins with lean teams.

**Dooley Tombras, CEO, Tombras**

*"We had a necessity to differentiate, because everybody in the industry looks at agencies the same way. Our differentiating point right now is that it's not easy to bolt together data plus creativity; we're still differentiated because we didn't bolt it together, we built it from the ground up."*

## Challenge 2: Know How to Be Found

You might be the perfect agency for a prospect in need, but that opportunity disappears if they can't find you. That's why understanding the customer journey is essential.

Marketers don't think about agencies until they must. They are focused on their own business, and because they think about agencies so rarely, their unaided awareness is very low. Even when they recognize an agency, their knowledge is minimal.

When we interview clients during an agency search, we ask which agencies they want us to consider. They can rarely name more than one or two. Often, they'll say things like "that Nike agency" or "the agency that did the Apple work." Most prospects simply don't know where to begin looking.

Clients don't read *Ad Age*, *Adweek*, or *Campaign* with the depth agency folks do. Even if they subscribe, they rarely consume those publications consistently. And their personal networks usually aren't much help. So they behave like most B2B buyers today: they research quietly, online, long before an agency knows they're looking.

What happens behind the scenes when a marketer needs to find a new agency? Typically, a middle manager is assigned the task of researching agencies and compiling a shortlist of potential candidates. Often, they start with a simple web search. A Google search for "advertising agencies" can return hundreds of millions of results. Even narrowing it down to something like "Seattle advertising agencies" still generates millions of hits.

Or they might turn to an AI tool to research the industry. In a market flooded with thousands of agencies, there's a good chance your agency won't even surface in the results of a search or AI prompt. Clearly, the odds are against any one agency.

But they don't have to be — there are steps agencies can take that will enhance their odds of being found when the right prospect is looking.

The key is to develop and execute a marketing plan that elevates your agency's brand.

By making strategic and focused choices, you can balance limited resources with the most impactful marketing efforts, whether that's submitting award applications, creating compelling content, engaging in PR, participating in trade shows, or securing speaking engagements.

While marketing your agency isn't the primary focus of this book, it's a critical foundation for why you need this book in the first place!

**Challenge 3: Pitch Well Once You're Found**

"Pitching" can take on many forms and meanings.

For our purposes, we're not focused simply on competitive opportunities. Rather, we are referring to any conversation you have as a representative of your agency that can yield new business. A conversation over coffee, an introduction at a conference, a call about something else that leads to a question about your agency. These all have the potential to lead to new business, so they can certainly be "pitches."

We've observed thousands of formal and informal pitches, and the unfortunate truth is that most of them end up looking the same — to us and to our clients.

These pitches often fail to excite or inspire the client or prospect. Someone wins simply because a decision has to be made — but it's frequently not the right agency, and sometimes not even the best one.

And most of the agencies that make it to a presentation

probably can do the work. They have the capability; that's how they got in the room. But it's a shame to see a good agency — the agency that has the strongest skillset to meet the prospect's specific needs — lose the prospect by not being properly prepared for or delivering a customer-centric pitch. And, unfortunately, there's little opportunity for an agency to learn what they've done wrong because they rarely, if ever, get a chance to receive any concrete, detailed feedback.

After sitting through thousands of pitches, we can tell you three main missteps account for most pitch failures:

1. **The agency is too focused on themselves.**

   When the agency focuses on themselves rather than the prospect, everyone loses.

   We've often witnessed agencies spend the first 20 minutes of a pitch talking about themselves, and then say, "Enough about us." Our thought is generally, "It was enough about you 20 minutes ago." Remember, you wouldn't be in the room if the prospect didn't already know enough about you to carve out valuable time for a presentation.

   And let's be clear: these meetings aren't about you in the first place, they're about the client's business. You set your agency apart by focusing on the client and demonstrating how you can help address their challenges, not by talking endlessly about your agency.

   Always remember that you bond with a prospect over their problem, not your solution.

**PROSPECT-FRIENDLY ACTIONS**

**Rob Davis, President, Novus Media**

*"Strategy is the art of deciding what not to do. It's easy to throw a lot of ideas and tactics around. What's hard is winnowing them down to only what will be most effective in addressing a specific business challenge. The most prospect-centric pitches don't just tell your story — they tell the prospect's story, better than they've heard it before."*

**2. The agency misses the mark by failing to address the prospect's key business issues.**

Agencies often fail to focus on the key business issues of the prospect.

Your incredible pitch and presentation are pointless if they don't tackle the prospect's real challenges. Remember, one is looking to buy advertising, PR, media, or digital marketing. But what they're really after is help solving their business problems. A strong focus on the prospect's business challenges helps convey thoughtfulness, expertise, and showcases that you understand their business. You "get" them.

Agency selection is an important *considered purchase* for a client. It is a risky decision. Clients can lose their jobs for hiring the wrong agency. Give them confidence that they are making a sound decision by showcasing how well you understand their challenges.

**PROSPECT-FRIENDLY ACTIONS**

**Jason Parks, Chief Growth Officer, BarkleyOKRP**

*"A winning pitch begins not with what we want to say, but with what the prospect really needs to win in the marketplace. The pitch solves a problem the prospect already feels."*

**3. The agency jumps straight to tactics instead of starting with strategy.**

Many agencies focus on tactics without having a strong strategy in place. This approach rarely works well.

When an agency leads with tactics, there is no logic to how to evaluate the tactics, nor whether they should work or not. Basically, the agency is asking the client to decide whether they like something without providing the criteria for evaluation.

The strategy is the benchmark for determining whether the tactics are effective. Strategy is the glue that connects the dots between the client's business challenge and your proposed solutions. It weaves a seamless narrative and provides the rationale for why your tactics will succeed.

**PROSPECT-FRIENDLY ACTIONS**

**Nicole Mahoney, CEO, Travel Alliance Partnership**

*"We're big on strategy, so we start everything with strategy first because we want to be able to deliver results. In one of our recent wins, the client loved the insight that we brought to her and the way we captured her market. We won a different account recently because the client said we understood his business and what his needs were. He appreciated our deep understanding of the industry and what he was trying to accomplish. He said to me that they finally felt like they were heard, and they felt like they weren't being sold to. They really felt like we understood them."*

### Win More Business

The world is evolving rapidly, and the agency landscape is in a perpetual state of disruption, impacting buyers, the purchasing process, and the competitive field. These challenges often result in agencies missing out on opportunities to win more than their fair share of pitches and secure new business. It doesn't have to be that way!

Keep reading, and we will help you with the key skills and approaches needed to win more than your fair share of new business opportunities.

## EXERCISE: AGENCY ANALYSIS

At the start of this journey, take some time to step back and consider the following:

1. Where does the majority of your new business come from?
2. Are you ready when a prospect approaches you?
3. Do you have a repeatable pitch process that wins new business more than a third of the time in competitive pitches?

# CHAPTER 2
# What Matters to Agency Prospects

There's a famous conversation in *The Wolf of Wall Street* that perfectly illustrates the mistakes many sellers make when trying to connect with a prospect. At a conference, Jordan Belfort (played by Leonardo DiCaprio) pulls a pen from his pocket and repeatedly challenges salespeople to sell it back to him. Each time, they stumble as they focus on describing the pen's features.

"It's an amazing pen. It's for, uh, professionals..."

"It's a nice pen. You can use the pen to write down thoughts from your life so you can remember what..."

"Well, this pen works and I personally love this pen..."

Jordan becomes increasingly frustrated as all of them fail at the task for the same reason that many agencies fail to woo clients and prospects: they're focused on the seller's wants and not the buyer's needs.

They're focused on the pen, not the prospect.

Remember, it's not about you!

**PROSPECT-FRIENDLY ACTIONS**

**Alex Nikdel, President, Echo Delta**

*"The core principle of every piece of marketing that we do is centered around making our prospects better at their jobs."*

## Lessons from "The Boss."

Remember the story of Bruce Springsteen and Jimmy Iovine from the introduction of this book?

Jon Landau looked Jimmy straight in the eye and said:

"You go back there and say to Bruce, 'I'm here to support you. This is not about me; it's about the album.' You do that and you will have a friend for life."

That story encapsulates the mindset agency executives need to adopt to succeed:

It's not about you.

## Talk Less and Listen More.

This mindset is about shifting how you view your clients and prospects.

Your mindset needs to be, "This isn't about me." We've sat on the client side of countless agency pitches and witnessed so many firms fail to grasp this. Every time, it's disheartening. We know agencies can improve simply by reframing their approach. As Bruce's manager advised, they need to focus on supporting the prospect, not on promoting themselves.

When it comes to agency success, our experience has shown that the most thriving agencies adopt the "It's not about me" mindset. They've mastered the art of truly understanding their clients' needs, driven by a genuine desire to make their lives easier and better.

Agency execs need to change their perspective from "Let me tell you how I can help you" to "Let me learn as much as I can about you so I know how I can best help you." It's a nuanced difference, but a difference indeed.

You've put in the effort to secure the meeting or get a prospect on the phone, and now it's happening. This initial conversation is crucial — it's a high-stakes moment often marked by a deep fear of rejection. This is the stage where the "I hate selling" mindset tends to creep in, making the risk feel greater than the reward. But that's not the case. It's your opportunity to demonstrate your value and credibility and to get permission to continue the conversation. To succeed, though, you need to drop the sales pitch, put down the bullhorn, and truly listen.

Many agencies are just too eager to get in and sell the prospect on the brilliance of their agency. They dive into talking about themselves, believing their skills and experience are the selling point. But they're not. Your credibility has no value if the prospect doesn't feel like you understand their challenge. If you're not patient enough to develop and understand the needs of the prospect, all you'll do is chest beat, which is not appealing, and you'll try to sell things that are generic because they're not tied to any specific insight.

**PROSPECT-FRIENDLY ACTIONS**

**Keitha Oliver, Pepper Advertising, Trinidad & Tobago**

*"I think what makes the difference is really understanding what the business issues are: the reason why the client is running the pitch. It's not just about creative, a pretty ad; it's a problem that they're trying to solve. I found that when we delve deeper into identifying what those business needs are and what the solutions are that they're really after, we've been able to use our experience to demonstrate why we may be the best candidates for the job."*

**Find Your In.**

To have a meaningful and impactful discussion with a prospect about their business, it's essential to have a clear understanding of their key business needs and challenges before you even step into the room. This takes serious preparation. To truly grasp the problems or opportunities a prospect is facing, you need to do your homework, so you know exactly what you're trying to solve. If you're too quick to jump in with, "I know how to grow your market share," you could easily lose the client before you even start. After all, they might not be concerned about market share at all — maybe their focus is on acquiring new customers.

To truly understand prospects, you need to grasp their business issues.

**PROSPECT-FRIENDLY ACTIONS**

**Carly Sabourin, Chief Client Officer, Think Shift**

*"Crafting a prospect-centric pitch that stands out is tough. It's tempting to skip the hard work and default to generic agency overviews and case studies that fail to connect. But investing time and effort to understand the prospect's business, pain points, and opportunities with thorough research and analysis makes all the difference. The right strategy will capture attention, spark engagement, and transform the pitch from a one-sided presentation into a dynamic conversation that sets the tone for a future partnership."*

### What is a business issue?

We define a business issue as the key challenges or opportunities a company is facing.

Business issues are not "nice to haves." They are clear and present dangers and prominent opportunities. They are discussed daily in the C-suite or owner's office. Business issues affect the company's bottom line and must be addressed for the company to grow and prosper.

Doing some homework on the likely business issues that

your prospect faces is job #1. Start by compiling a list of what you believe the prospect's business issues might be, based on what you already know, what they've shared with you, and what you can uncover through desk research. Your task here is to use your research tools to help pinpoint the prospect's potential business issues. It's a bit of a guessing game at this stage, because you'll need to confirm these assumptions once you get the chance to have a conversation with the client or prospect.

Here's a list of the most common opportunities and challenges that we see across most businesses today. By no means is this exhaustive, but it should give you a good starting point from which to create your own list.

**Business and Brand Success Factors**

- *Is the prospect's revenue going up or down?*
- *How profitable is the prospect?*
- *What is the prospect's current brand image?*
- *Are there unmet expectations?*

**Business Initiatives**

- *Are there products new to the market or on the horizon?*
- *How did the target audience receive any recent launches?*
- *What did recent turnaround calendars look like?*
- *Have they recently done any re-positioning?*

**Customer Behaviors**

- *Why do customers purchase the brand?*
- *What is their current customer relationship like?*
- *How much is the average customer spending?*
- *Are there up-sell or cross-sell opportunities?*
- *What is the current churn rate?*

### Marketing Measures

- *How strong is unaided and aided awareness of the brand?*
- *What do prospects think and feel about the brand?*
- *What is foot traffic and digital traffic like at their stores and websites?*
- *How much channel support exists?*

### Organizational Issues

- *What is the quality of the product or service?*
- *What is the culture like at the prospect's company?*
- *How engaged are the employees in the company?*
- *What is the morale level like at the company?*
- *Are there technology issues that need to be addressed with regard to how the prospect is doing business?*

Remember, the list above is just a starting point. Business issues are the core challenges or opportunities a prospect's organization may be facing, and the potential list can be lengthy.

Having a sound idea of the most likely business issues is critical, because that list sets you up for important discussions with your prospect. If you can acknowledge the real challenge, the client will start to see you as a possible ally, which changes everything.

### The Ulta Beauty Example

As an example, on March 12, 2020, Ulta Beauty published a press release titled "Ulta Beauty Announces Fourth Quarter Fiscal 2019 Results" that was filled with pertinent information useful to any marketing agency. Some notable selections:

"We knew the fourth quarter would be challenging given both the category headwinds and the fact that we are lapping a very strong quarter last year," said CEO Mary Dillon.

**For Q4 2019:**

- Net sales increased by 8.5%
- Comparable sales increased by 4.0%

**For 2019:**

- Net sales increased by 10.1%
- Gross profit as a percentage of net sales increased 30 basis points
- SG&A expenses as a percentage of net sales increased 90 basis points

**And coming up in 2020, Ulta Beauty was projecting:**

- Opening approximately 75 net new stores, executing approximately 15 remodel or relocation projects, and completing approximately 42 store refreshes

When we put on our business development hat, what does this press release tell us?

At a glance, we know how incredibly successful Ulta Beauty has been. More than 8.5% sales growth in Q4 compared very favorably to all retail results in 4Q 2019. We see that while net profit increased, so did SG&A — suggesting increased efficiency may be important in the future. And we see that they plan on opening 75 new stores and completing many remodels, which would require marketing support. This important information, readily available to the public, can help inform an agency regarding the situation at Ulta Beauty and help prepare the agency for further discussions.

Consider how different an exploratory conversation would be with Ulta Beauty if you had prepared with this better understanding of their potential business issues. Ulta Beauty had a great holiday season yet continued to face core beauty industry headwinds. That is a very different outlook and basis for conversation than simply admiring the fine results.

## Figuring It Out

There are numerous ways to uncover a prospect's business issues — many of which are right in front of you, whether in the RFP or in the news. If they're not immediately obvious, you can develop a deeper understanding with a bit of effort. Your role during the prospecting and pitch process is to continue to build an understanding of what the business issues are in the eyes of the prospect, and then (and only then) to showcase how your agency can uniquely help the prospect solve those challenges and opportunities.

A clear understanding of a prospect's situation can help you create a relevant and memorable pitch. Earlier, we mentioned a scene from *The Wolf of Wall Street* where Leonardo DiCaprio's Jordan Belfort flustered sales agents with the seemingly simple task of selling him a pen. In a later scene, Jordan returns to the example when a coworker claims he can sell anything to anyone. But when Jordan tells him to sell the pen, the guy hesitates with uncertainty. Jordan gives the pen to a friend of his who replies with a quick, "Write your name down on that napkin for me." To which Jordan replies, "I don't have a pen." And his friend tosses the pen on the table. "Exactly. Supply and demand, my friend."

Only the person who pinpointed and addressed the buyer's actual needs delivered the winning pitch.

The key is to remember it's not about you! It's about the prospect and their business. In the end, you won't win every pitch, but by shifting your approach to focus first on the prospect's needs, you might sell a few more pens.

---

## EXERCISE: PROSPECT RESEARCH

Consider three prospects you'd love to have as clients. Don't worry too much about the feasibility of landing such clients, just pick three that really interest you. Now research them more fully than you have in the past and make a list of possible business issues for each. Ask yourself:

- In what industry category/categories is their company?
- What products and/or services do they offer?
- Who are their target customers?
- How do they find new customers?
- What are the biggest challenges they face in achieving success?
- What are their overarching goals as a company?
- What are their top priorities or concerns?

# CHAPTER 3
# Getting on the List

A few years ago, we noticed a serious gap in the approach agencies were taking to guide their business development plans and activities. There was no documented knowledge base regarding the buyer journey for agency services.

Extensive research has been conducted on customer journeys across countless industries and categories — much of it led by agencies themselves. Yet, surprisingly, no one had examined the journey of the buyer of agency services.

So, we took it upon ourselves to explore it.

This information is critical to your firm's planning, strategies, pipeline, and new business win rate. Here's what we learned.

The buyer's journey for agency services unfolds across six distinct stages.

The Customer Journey for Agency Services

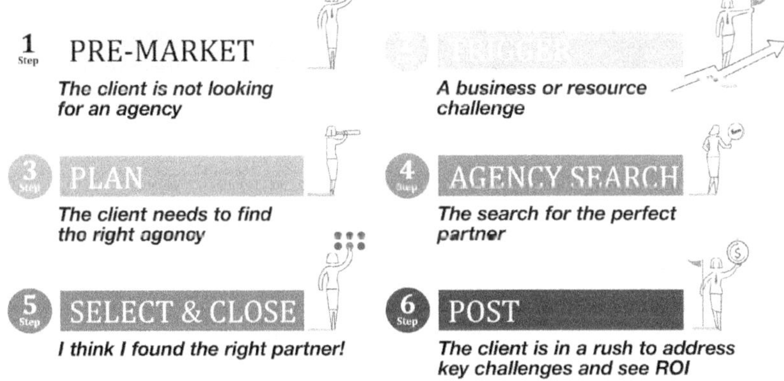

*Let's review these steps.*

### Step 1: Pre-Market

What's happening: The client isn't actively searching for an agency. They're focused on their own business and daily life. They have limited knowledge of the agency landscape, don't keep tabs on agencies, and, frankly, don't care much about them. They might subscribe to *Ad Age* or *Adweek*, but they don't religiously follow these publications to stay updated on the agency world.

Instead, they are focused on their business and building their knowledge and expertise to support it. They are focused on their business and their career.

When they do take a break from the business challenges at hand, they focus their business-related reading and video watching on advancing their business and functional knowledge. They read business publications and trade and industry journals. They might attend industry shows/ virtual conferences and maybe an ANA conference. They aren't thinking about or reading about agencies.

So, with key client decision-makers focused on their own business and not giving agencies a second thought, what should your goals be at this stage? Keep in mind, this is the phase where clients spend most of their time — and they simply don't know many agencies by name. Unaided awareness is extremely low.

Succeeding at this stage is incredibly challenging. Your objectives at this stage are to:

- Build awareness
- Enhance your reputation
- Grow your database — your key audience — so you're prepared to engage with them throughout the rest of their journey.

To win at this stage, the agency's focus must be on "readiness," ensuring the agency:

- Is clearly and distinctively positioned
- Has a prospect-friendly website
- Is easily "findable"
- Prioritizes limited resources to elevate awareness and reputation

An agency's growth depends upon this step in the journey.

We've studied the buyer's behaviors and identified the actions agencies need to take to ensure they're ready when clients begin their search. We'd be happy to discuss this in more detail with any agency.

**Step 2: Trigger**

In this step, the client/prospect has been triggered. A trigger is a change to the marketer's situation that causes them to rethink the status quo. The trigger is almost always a change or a challenge. Changes can include new leadership, new channels, or new strategies. They could be opportunities, like a new product launch. Challenges can include poor business results, new or enhanced competition, or even poor agency performance.

At this stage, they are concerned, and they know they need to respond to the trigger. What does the agency need to do at this step?

There's not much you can do about the trigger if you're unaware it occurred — and most of the time you won't even know it has. In the handful of cases where you are aware of the trigger, direct outreach may be successful.

**Step 3: Plan**

Having been triggered by a change or challenge, the client needs to find the right agency. They know they need help...

but they don't know where or how to find that help.

Remember, they don't follow the agency world. They don't know of many agencies and have little time to learn on their own, given their day-to-day business challenges. At this point, they are overwhelmed and generally do one of three things:

- Delegate the task
- Do it themselves
- Hire a consultant (in about 20% of agency reviews, and mostly the larger ones)

There are steps an agency can take to seize opportunities during this stage, but the chances of success are significantly higher if the agency has excelled in Step 1 with distinction. Your task at this point is straightforward: you need to get on the list. The odds, however, of making that list are slim if you haven't proactively addressed Step 1.

### Step 4: Agency Search

By step 4, the client has begun the search for the perfect agency partner. The prospect is formally or informally searching. It could be a middle manager, a senior executive or owner, or a consultant. At this stage, they are determined to find the right partner to help them address their business challenge or opportunity.

At this stage they generally conduct some of the following:

- Agency research
- RFI
- Q&A calls
- Briefings
- RFP
- Chemistry sessions

- Formal presentations
- Cost proposals
- References

Your goal at this stage is to win the pitch! The agency mindset at this stage should remain prospect focused.

### Step 5: Select & Close

The client believes they've found the right partner. They want to feel confident in their decision and may need to build buy-in from others (management, etc.). The prospect wants to feel good about the agreement they're making. At this stage, they're experiencing a mix of nervousness, relief, and excitement. Your objective at this stage is to:

- Build the prospect's confidence in their decision
- Make it easy for them to say "yes"
- Create an emotional connection

The agency mindset at this stage should center on making the process smooth and welcoming. Approach the process with grace by offering solutions that benefit both parties, demonstrating that you're an easy, collaborative partner to work with.

### Step 6: Post

Invariably, the client is in a rush to address their challenges and see impact. The prospect urgently needs to get going.

- They need to onboard the agency effectively, but don't know how or have the time
- There may be an agency transition that must be managed
- The client is focused on their business challenges and is impatient to make headway

At this stage, they are focused on getting results. Your objective is to get going quickly!

- Build the relationship
- Deliver initial assignments ahead of schedule, below budget, and with distinction

The agency mindset at this stage is all about showing appreciation and enthusiasm. Thank the client and dive into the work without delay.

### *In Summary*

The agency prospect's customer journey consists of six steps. While every step is crucial for your agency's success, excelling at Step 1 is by far your best strategy for building a stronger pipeline and getting more opportunities. Mastering the remaining steps is then essential if you want to win more of those opportunities.

For this book, we will assume your agency has built the awareness and reputation necessary to be included in pitch opportunities. Our focus will be on helping your agency win the opportunities when they arise.

---

## EXERCISE: YOUR KNOWLEDGE OF THE CUSTOMER JOURNEY

Reflect on these questions:

- Do you have strategies in place to address each step of the customer journey?
- What strategies have you tried to increase your number of opportunities?
- Of those strategies, what has worked, and what hasn't?

# CHAPTER 4
# Readiness

You've studied the customer journey and are actively building your agency's brand effectively.

You're starting to attract inbound interest!

Prospects are reaching out to your agency — great progress!

They're eager to learn more and see if you can help them tackle their challenges.

To capitalize on that outreach from prospects, you need to be prepared.

And you need to be ready in a prospect-friendly way.

Readiness involves several key steps, which we'll explore in the upcoming chapters:

- Agency positioning
- Case studies
- A prospect-friendly website
- A prospect-friendly response template

We'll dive into these essential readiness steps in the next few chapters.

With these readiness activities in place, you'll be fully prepared for the next inbound opportunity.

# CHAPTER 5
# Readiness Tools:
# Agency Positioning

Every day, across the globe, agencies are working hard to differentiate their clients and help drive their clients' growth. These agencies use the art and science of positioning to help their clients stand out from the competition.

Pretzels are pretzels. Peanut butter is peanut butter. Yet, different companies have found ways to position their products so that some stand out more than others. For example, there are countless sneakers, but there's only one Nike. There are many mobile phones, but there's only one iPhone. There's ice cream, and then there's Ben & Jerry's.

Levi's.

Starbucks.

Snickers.

Target.

McDonalds.

There are campaigns that transform brands into unforgettable and compelling icons, like *Just Do It*, *Taste the Rainbow*, and *Because You're Worth It*.

The list goes on and on of brands that rise above their competitors. We know you're aware of this. The real question is: how can you apply these same principles to your own agency?

As Mischief's Oliver McAteer has said:

"Agencies need to act like brands."

Sadly, most agencies don't act like brands.

Most agencies doing fine work for the clients have not worked the same positioning magic for themselves despite competing with thousands of other agencies. The world has an abundance of talented and effective agencies that have failed to distinguish themselves, and they are missing out on the significant and very profitable growth opportunities triggered by compelling and distinctive agency brand positioning.

If you're trying to figure out how to build your agency's business, you have to figure out how to stand out.

Proper positioning is a vital step in that direction. Your agency needs to be distinctive enough to stand out and avoid blending into the crowd.

**PROSPECT-FRIENDLY ACTIONS**

**Jarrett Smith, VP of Strategy, Echo Delta**

*"If I were to give one piece of advice about new business development, it's got to be all about positioning. That is the lead domino. Many agencies are not positioned effectively. And until you solve that problem, you're just going into a headwind. Once you solve the positioning problem, everything gets a lot easier, from how to train and develop your staff and who to hire to which conference to attend, and what to write on your blog. The wind is at your back."*

---

## DISTINCTIVENESS TIPS FOR YOUR AGENCY

As you work toward defining your agency's distinctiveness, keep these three key points in mind:

**1. It has to be about more than your people.**

We've often heard agencies say, "You know what makes our agency different? Our people."

That simply is not compelling enough.

Prospects will naturally assume you have a strong team. Without a solid team, you wouldn't have made it on their radar in the first place — it's unlikely you would have produced any noteworthy work without the right talent in your agency.

If you can say "We have the *Got Milk*? guy" or "our creative team has won four Emmys and 30 Lions," you can add credibility to your agency. But even those claims are not your positioning. They are about you.

Remember: it's not about you.

**2. Make it clear.**

We once heard an agency describe themselves as "a transformation design agency."

The statement served as both their frame of reference (what kind of agency they are) and their positioning (what makes them distinct).

It failed on both counts.

What does "we're a transformation design agency" even mean?

It might be distinctive, but it's not important to your target audience if they don't understand it.

Your positioning statement can't just be a clever statement that makes you feel good. It needs to be meaningful, easily understood, and compelling to your target audience. Your prospect is searching for real solutions to their actual problems.

In the example above, we helped them land on the much more succinct "retail marketing agency" as their frame of reference. It's crystal clear who they are and what they do. Shortly after making this change, they received a significant RFP for a retail marketing assignment, which they ultimately won.

3. **Take your own advice.**

   Many agencies have experience meeting with clients or prospects who claim their company, challenge, or business is completely unique. This is rarely, if ever, the case.

   It's the same with agencies. They're seldom as unusual as they think they are, so it's important to take the same advice you give to your clients. Take an honest look at how you stack up against the competition. Examine who you really are. Figure out what is really important to your customers or clients. From there, you can start to define your agency in ways that distinctively speak to prospects' needs.

   You must find a way to talk about yourself that helps a potential client think, "Wow, these guys might actually be worth listening to" or "I can see the difference between Agency You and Agency Them."

### PROSPECT-FRIENDLY ACTIONS

**Janet Casey, Managing Partner, Gravity Global**

*"Positioning your agency has never been more critical. In today's crowded market, distinctiveness is your ticket to the dance. Within one minute on your website, prospects should understand exactly what you do best and what it's like to work with you. Fresh, outside perspectives are invaluable in ensuring your positioning is accurate and full of life."*

It's nearly impossible for an agency to be truly *differentiated* today. There are too many agencies, and regardless of an agency's focus and capabilities, there are likely hundreds, if not thousands, of agencies that can do the same work in roughly the same way.

Instead of differentiation, the goal is to create a little white space around your brand, as iconic agencies of the past did. To be *distinctive*.

## Lesson From the Great Agencies of Old

Most agencies today face the challenge of how to effectively position their firm and how to present their agency in a compelling, customer-centric manner. It was not always like this!

Iconic agencies of the past were distinctive in how they presented themselves to the world. We knew what Young & Rubicam was and how that was different from J. Walter Thompson. It was obvious how McCann was different from Grey. The distinctiveness in how these agencies were positioned helped drive growth.

But how exactly did they do it, and how does it apply to your agency?

## Benton & Bowles

Remember Benton & Bowles? If you're not familiar, Benton & Bowles was the agency that pioneered the radio soap opera. They leveraged their expertise in soap operas to position themselves as the agency that understood the housewife, the primary shopper for most families.

By 1936, Benton & Bowles was producing three of the top four radio soap operas. They continued to evolve and build upon this distinctiveness by working with Procter & Gamble to launch *As the World Turns* on television in

1956. The soap opera audiences were homemakers who were sneaking in their "stories" as an escape from the responsibilities of doing laundry, cleaning the bathroom, and preparing dinner. They were always on the lookout for quick meal ideas, cleaning solutions, and beauty supplies.

If your business wanted to reach these soap opera audiences, Benton & Bowles was the solution.

### Leo Burnett

Leo Burnett had a different point of view. Leo believed that the essence of great advertising was in capturing the inherent drama of the product being advertised.

To achieve this, he used archetypes — often embodied by characters he created — to humanize the product's inherent drama in a unique and unforgettable way. You knew exactly what you were getting when you hired Leo Burnett! The agency brought to life iconic characters like the Pillsbury Doughboy, the Jolly Green Giant, Charlie the Tuna, Tony the Tiger, the Keebler Elves, Toucan Sam, the Maytag Repairman, the Marlboro Man, and many others.

### Ogilvy

David Ogilvy was the scientist marketer. He started his career as a pollster, working for Gallup. When World War II broke out, he served in British intelligence, using his analytical skills to support the Allies' war effort.

Following the war, he started his own advertising agency with a straightforward premise: that the function of advertising was to sell. His agency brought science and data-driven thinking to that belief. He also thought that the best approach to new business was to do well by your current clients — that great work was your best calling card.

The timeless classic book *Ogilvy on Advertising* brings this compelling philosophy to life and extra momentum to the agency's differentiation and success.

### Doyle Dane Bernbach

Bill Bernbach of Doyle Dane Bernbach was essentially the anti-Ogilvy. He believed that persuasion was not about science, but rather about art. He believed in simple, dramatic advertising. VW advertising created by his agency, like "Lemon" and "Think Small," are great examples of this philosophy.

### Today?

Today, advertisers struggle to distinguish most agencies from onc another. While a small group of agencies has managed to build a brand around the quality of their creative work, the majority blend into the crowd.

Occasionally an agency will stand out.

If someone is even remotely aware of the marketing industry, they know the work and reputation of Wieden+Kennedy.

Often referred to as "the Nike agency," Wieden+Kennedy is consistently hailed as one of the best creative agencies in the world, a reputation solidified by their annual recognition with major creative awards and business wins. Not only that, but in 2019, their creative leader, Colleen DeCourcy, was named AdWeek Creative Leader of the Decade.

Beyond Wieden+Kennedy, there are a handful of other agencies that manage to stand out.

GS&P redefined creative marketing with the *Got Milk?* juggernaut.

And BBDO was named "Most Strategic Network in the World" five years in a row.

And today, Mischief is commonly hailed as a possible successor to the throne of the greatest creative agency in the world.

Most agencies never reach that level of acclaim and cannot count on the uniqueness of their work to help them stand out. This lack of distinctiveness represents an enormous opportunity for most agencies, but it's often approached incorrectly. Many aspire to the same level of acclaim as an agency like Wieden+Kennedy, but you can't stand out by trying ALSO to be the best creative agency in the world. That is a singular positioning that only one agency can own, and it's already taken.

Why aim to be just another "also" when you can become "the one and only"?

Here's what you can do.

### The DASP and Enhanced Agency Positioning

The foundation of an effective agency growth strategy is a compelling agency positioning — what we call a "DASP" (Distinctive Agency Selling Proposition) — that clearly defines your agency to the outside world. As we discussed in Chapter 1, agencies face numerous challenges in today's market. There is, however, an opportunity to tackle these challenges by positioning your agency in a truly compelling and distinctive way.

We've studied agency positioning and identified several key elements essential for success.

### The Starting Point — What Kind of Agency Are You?

Many agencies forget about a critical element of brand positioning when it comes to their own brand. Just what kind of agency are they positioning?

This critical gap leads to agencies missing out on business opportunities every single day.

In classic brand positioning work, the two core elements are captured by defining "the type of product or service" being positioned and "what makes the product or service special?"

## Frame of Reference

We refer to the kind of product or service as the brand's "frame of reference." This helps define what category the brand belongs to and determines which products or services it should be compared with. For example, consider granola in a supermarket. What section would you expect to find it in? In the cereal aisle, of course. While granola can serve a multitude of other purposes, from being a baking ingredient to a snack to a dessert topping, its primary use is cereal. And therefore, you will find it in the cereal section.

This definition is critical. It helps consumers find a brand and compare it to similar products. This illustrates how a frame of reference groups products together based on shared characteristics.

And just as important as this frame of reference notion is to a consumer product, it may be even more important to agencies. Clients and prospects typically have very, very low unaided awareness of agency brands. When they search for agencies to consider, they generally start by defining the "type" of agency they need — what we call frame of reference.

There are several widely recognized frames of reference in the agency landscape, each corresponding to a distinct type of agency. Common examples include:

- Creative agency
- Media agency
- PR (public relations) agency
- Full-service advertising agency
- Digital marketing agency
- Shopper marketing agency
- Brand design agency
- Social agency
- Influencer agency

These categories help clarify the agency's primary area of expertise and indicate which other agencies they should be compared to within the market.

Keep in mind, this aspect of an agency's positioning does not set it apart or make it distinctive. Instead, it serves as a point of commonality that allows potential clients to identify and locate the agency.

Certain agencies clearly define their frame of reference:

- New Engen identifies as a digital marketing agency.
- Porter Novelli describes itself as a communications and public relations firm.
- Curiosity positions itself as a full-service creative agency.
- Horizon is known as a media agency.

Others are less explicit, failing to clearly state on their homepage — or elsewhere — the type of agency they are.

Some can be quite unusual. For example, have you ever come across a "transformation design agency?" Neither had we, until some friends used that term to describe their retail shopper agency.

Try this exercise: pick any agency and visit their website. Does the homepage, within the first visible section, clearly state the agency's frame of reference? My guess is that if you check five agencies, only one or two will clearly define it. This is unfortunate for both the agency and its potential clients.

When positioning your agency to be distinctive and memorable, make sure to clearly define its type. You want your agency to be compared with others, but you also want to control the category in which it is compared!

### Three Essential Elements of Distinctive Positioning

After establishing the frame of reference, three crucial elements of effective positioning can help any agency stand out and achieve lasting success:

1. A compelling **agency philosophy** that inspires both clients and employees, instilling confidence that the quality of work will match the agency's proven track record.

2. An insight-driven **strategic process** that brings strategy to life through impactful work, providing a strong reason to believe the agency can solve the client's challenges.

3. An **interaction process** that fosters client engagement and builds ownership and confidence in the agency's work.

Let's take a closer look at each.

### Elements of a Great Agency Philosophy

The purpose of a clearly defined agency philosophy is to instill confidence in the agency's work. It gives the agency a unified voice shared by everyone on the staff and creates a singular message to the marketplace. This philosophy serves as the creative expression of the agency's distinctiveness and can shape:

- How the agency defines success
- What the agency considers good work
- What sets the agency apart from competitors
- How the agency motivates and inspires its staff

### Agency Philosophy in Practice

Let's start at the beginning. In 1912, McCann defined themselves with another classic example of a powerful agency philosophy:

**Truth Well Told**

Three powerful words: Truth Well Told.

This positioning has remained unchanged for over a century — and for good reason. It's simply outstanding.

It starts with "Truth," so we know that what they do is based on fact. Businesses can understand the importance of truth for them and their business results. And "Well Told" is the creative part. It's the storytelling. Together, the agency is promising both truth and art.

They've never needed to change it because it was flawless and perfectly fitting.

Goodby Silverstein & Partners (GS&P) has been well-known for many years for great business-driven creative. That creative work is the product of the leadership of ad legends Jeff Goodby and Rich Silverstein.

Years ago, Jeff crafted a manifesto-style statement capturing the agency's philosophy. We consider it one of the finest ever written:

**Art Serving Capitalism**

In just three words, you grasp their entire approach. GS&P's work isn't acceptable unless it qualifies as art — and it must also deliver business results. They set an exceptionally high standard and went even further by pairing their philosophy with an equally powerful mantra. It's brilliant writing backed by brilliant thinking.

*"Capitalism, for the most part, distrusts art.*

*But a look at history shows that business has been at its best when it's done with the sense of craft and surprise we associate with art.*

*Art is the stutter step that freezes the opponent. It's a new way of seeing the world that takes things that are basically the same and makes them suddenly seem different. Art takes things that don't belong together and welds them at high temperatures. Art teaches business to dance.*

*At Goodby, Silverstein & Partners, there is no doubt that we are capitalists. We love business. But we believe that it is most successfully accomplished with the help of art. And this faith has made all the difference. For us, and for our clients. We believe that art is the secret weapon of great business. It is what makes the deaf suddenly hear, what makes the blind see. Notice, however that we are interested in making art that serves capitalism. We like keeping score. We like to win. We like the clarity of it. In the end, art combined with business is bigger art. Business combined with art is bigger business."*

Results from embracing this philosophy? Iconic campaigns like:

- *Got Milk?*
- Foster Farms' Chicken Imposters
- Denny's Free Grand Slam Day
- Budweiser's Lizards
- *There Can Only Be One* NBA Campaign
- ...along with countless other campaigns that drive real business success

## PROSPECT-FRIENDLY ACTIONS

**Jeff Goodby, Co-Chairman, GS&P**

*"It's not a big idea to start an advertising agency. People start them all the time. We have to do something different to really make this worthwhile. It has to be unlike any other one around. How are you going to do that? Rich and I came up with the Art Serving Capitalism phrase back in the late 80s or early 90s. It had a tiny bit of tongue in cheek to it. It's not art serving business — we chose the word capitalism. Art serving capitalism is a little funny. There's a tension to it. It says making money in a little bit more edgy way. We're not afraid of that. I think it was a warning to clients and an invitation to get engaged, to do something big, to do work that might appeal to people more like art does. There's an intent to it. It's supposed to get a rise out of people, get them to do something, get them to think, move them emotionally. As Howard Gossage said, 'Boring advertising works fine. It's really a choice to make advertising that's interesting, which works.' It's a choice."*

---

Tombras adopted a different yet equally clear approach:

**Connecting Data + Creativity for Business Results**

This statement clearly defines their identity and resonates with their target audience. Business results take center stage, and they have invested significantly in developing a robust system that leverages data to enhance their advertising.

When Dooley Tombras took over the company from his father, he said, "Dad, we have to invest in technology. We're not going to be able to advance if we're not data-driven, and we must have the technology to be able to be data-driven." That commitment became a reality and was even incorporated into the company's philosophy.

These agencies are not alone. Firms such as TBWA\Chiat\Day ("The disruption company.") and others have discovered that a compelling agency philosophy both inspires their clients and energizes their teams.

## Elements of a Great Strategic Process

With a compelling philosophy established, the next step is developing a repeatable system that consistently produces brilliant, insightful, and successful work.

The purpose of a clear strategic process is to give clients and prospects a reason to believe that your agency has a system that works time and time again. This begins by building a proven track record of solving client-specific business challenges, offering concrete evidence of a client-first approach that prioritizes understanding their needs above all else. Such a process:

- Starts with addressing the client's business issue
- Considers critical contexts, including brand, category, and consumer
- Aligns with the agency's culture and agency philosophy
- Delivers value beyond the agency's immediate scope
- Inspires exceptional work

## Implementing the Strategic Process

Pinnacle Advertising is a fine agency that lives by an intriguing philosophy: *The creative pursuit of serious results.* They are serious about a client's business results and use exceptional creativity to help clients succeed. Their 2025 Super Bowl commercial for WeatherTech is one of the strongest Super Bowl ads ever tested by System1.

To get to such fine work, the agency has a disciplined strategic process:

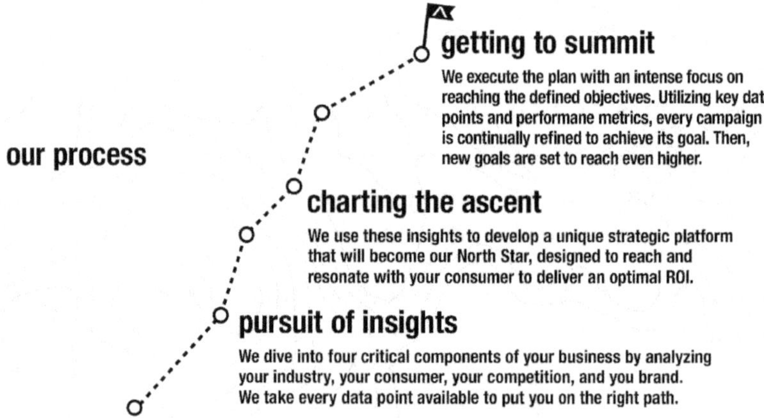


The process is clear, disciplined, thorough and flows naturally from the agency's name and philosophy.

**PROSPECT-FRIENDLY ACTIONS**

**Mark Figliulo, Founder and Creative Chairman, FIG**

*"Storytellers for the Information Age is our philosophy and One Story, Many Voices is how we do it. There's so much information today and everything got so fragmented. There's so many channels now. Everything was pulled apart because there's so much access to information now that we felt you needed to bring it back into one thing. Marketers were doing one thing on TV and another thing online and another thing on their website. It was all different stories. We felt that clients needed their one story, that one true thing that they stand for. So it's a story being told in many different ways and a lot of different timings, but it's the same story."*

## Elements of a Great Interaction Philosophy

A compelling agency philosophy mixed with terrific people and an insight-driven process can produce great work. Getting from good ideas to a great client relationship or from good raw thinking to work approved and in market, however, is not an afterthought. Rather, the most successful agencies also have client interaction processes that invite the client into the process and engage the client in the outcome, thereby creating co-ownership.

The interaction philosophy describes what it is like for a client to work with the agency. Typically, an interaction philosophy is:

- Client-centric
- Values-based
- Aligned with the agency's philosophy and strategic process
- Focused on delivering client benefits

It's important to understand that these values aren't just publicly displayed — they are shared internally to ensure the entire team is aligned. This document defines what the agency values and what it's like to work with the agency. The purpose of the interaction philosophy is to communicate aspects of your agency that are relevant and meaningful to your prospects and clients.

### PROSPECT-FRIENDLY ACTIONS

**Mark Figliulo, Founder and Creative Chairman, FIG**

*"We picked one value as our main focus and not just a whole set of words that you don't understand. And it doesn't mean we only have one value, it just means if we get this one right, it sets the stage for everything else. We chose telling the truth. It starts with telling the truth to each other. We said it immediately to anybody we hired, so I think if you guys sat down with everybody in our agency, you'd be shocked at how much everybody at the agency knows everything. And the logical extension is that we tell the truth to a client. It sounds so easy, but it's so hard to do. It sometimes takes a lot of courage to tell a client the truth."*

## Interaction Process in Practice

Years ago, Kaplan Thaler Group developed an excellent interaction philosophy. The team frequently highlighted their book, *The Power of Nice*, in their presentations.

This book set the Kaplan Thaler Group experience apart from other agencies. In their own words:

> *"A core philosophy of our agency is that we should be the best part of our client's day. We know there are many not-so-fun things our clients have to deal with on a regular basis. The creative and the agency should be two of the most enjoyable things.*
>
> *We believe N-I-C-E is the most powerful four-letter word in the English language. It is at the heart of who we are, how we treat each other, how we work with our clients, and how we create loyal relationships with consumers.*
>
> *All this translates to a culture of building up, not tearing down. Support, not isolation. And collaborative interaction, not pride of authorship. It starts from the top and trickles down to everyone at the agency."*

## Bringing It All Together

When an agency positions itself effectively, it becomes immediately clear who the agency is best suited to serve. This clarity benefits both potential clients and prospective employees, allowing everyone to understand exactly what to expect before any interaction begins.

You can't confidently promote yourself without first defining who you are. Put in the effort up front so you can earn the work.

---

### The Story Behind Tombras' Connecting Data + Creativity for Business Results

We talked to Dooley Tombras, CEO of Tombras, about his agency's positioning. A born storyteller, it made sense to let him share the journey in his own words.

> *"Really, it started in about 2010 for us. I think that it was not one thing. It was a lot of little signals that I was seeing where basically it felt like we were at an inflection point as an industry, meaning that digital had been second fiddle up to that point, and clients had creative agencies and they had digital agencies, and the digital budgets were typically a lot smaller than the brand creative budgets.*
>
> *Then the recession happened in '08 and '09, and everybody had to get scrappy. Agencies had to get scrappy, clients had to get scrappy. I just started to get the feeling that in 2010, hey, everything has just changed. The industry's not recognizing it yet, but digital actually just went from being secondary to arguably being primary, because of share of eyeballs. The eyeballs were now all on mobile, and they were all on social.*
>
> *I saw it as a huge opportunity, as an independent agency in the middle of the country, not in a major ad market, to differentiate and go all in on digital, because primarily we were not competing against small digital agencies. We were competing against bigger brand creative agencies, and CMOs didn't view us, quite often, as being differentiated enough to stick their neck out on the chopping block and take a risk to hire an independent in Tennessee. We'd get into pitches, but we just couldn't quite win.*
>
> *We wanted to go all in on digital, and the beauty of digital was that it was measurable. I was also detecting a trend where CMOs were under a lot of pressure in 2010 to start to show ROI, because CEOs were starting to hold them*

*accountable. CEOs were going to conferences and reading articles about how digital marketing was measurable, and they were wanting to hold their CMOs accountable to attribution and measurability.*

*Marketing had not been nearly as measured up to that point. It had been a lot softer KPIs and softer metrics about brand tracking studies and brand affinity and lift in aided and unaided awareness, but marketing had not been as accountable one-to-one to sales as it probably should have been, just as an industry, up to that point.*

*We decided to reposition the agency around Connecting Data + Creativity for Business Results, and make a big investment. We put a lot of poker chips in as an independent, family-owned company to invest in data and analytics. We made that the core of the agency and became a 'modern agency' rather than a digital agency, because we saw the future of the industry as leaning fully digital.*

*We wanted to stay really strong in strategic planning and creative, but we wanted to be 50/50 traditional and digital. We did it, not thinking that we would profit and not expecting to grow like we did. We did it because we just thought it was the right thing to do to help clients get better business results, because the consumer's share of attention was going to digital and to mobile. If you do that, you ought to be able to make it measurable.*

*Of course, there's a flywheel effect. Win some bigger clients, get a little bit better revenue, be able to attract a little bit better talent to Knoxville, and we can pay better salaries, and we've got better brands for people to work on. Then with that better talent, we're able to win more clients. That flywheel effect kept going, and here we are today."*

---

## EXERCISE: YOUR AGENCY'S POSITION

Challenge yourself with these questions:

- Does your agency have a clear frame of reference?
- Is the frame of reference clearly stated on the agency's homepage?
- Does your positioning distinctively identify what makes your agency special?
- Do you have an agency process?
- Does your agency have a distinctive way to talk about what it is like for clients to work with the agency?

# CHAPTER 6
# Readiness Tools: Case Studies

Case studies are important tools in an agency's business development process.

In our work, we often see cases that only tell part of the story, miss key elements, or are simply uninteresting. And we see agencies often send "canned" case studies that either lack relevance, or the relevance is not obvious.

We've analyzed countless case studies and have actionable suggestions to elevate yours. Case studies are essential for winning new business: they provide tangible proof of your success and build confidence in your agency's strategy and skills.

**PROSPECT-FRIENDLY ACTIONS**

**Ashley Walters, Partner & CMO, Curiosity**

*"Case studies aren't just proof, they're persuasion. They're one of the most powerful tools you have to win new business, but only if you make the connection between your work and their world obvious from the first page. A running shoe has nothing to do with a cruise line... until it does. The magic isn't just in showing category relevance. It's also proving how you solved similar business problems, or reached the same target audience, or even how you thrived in a similar company culture. Find the overlap with their brief and spotlight it. Don't make them work for it. Make it impossible to miss."*

Don't be intimidated by case studies. The secret is to view them from your prospect's point of view. Instead of simply highlighting your success, create a template that shows potential clients how you can solve their business problems. Include the details that will lead them to "yes."

In practical terms, case studies are often best drafted by someone who worked on the account, or failing that, someone who can ask questions of those who did. In any case, appoint someone who knows the agency's format and the project background, and of course, it wouldn't hurt if they can tell a good story.

**PROSPECT-FRIENDLY ACTIONS**

**Nicole Mahoney, CEO, Travel Alliance Partnership**

*"We needed to identify a champion within our team to make it happen."*

### Elements of a Good Case Study

While visual appeal and brand consistency are important, the true power of a case study lies in its narrative. To craft a compelling story, include these five key elements:

**1. The Challenge:**

Clearly define the client's business issues, marketing challenges, and key objectives.

**2. Analysis & Insight:**

Describe the research you conducted and your analysis of the client's brand, audience, and competitive landscape. This section reveals the crucial insight that drove your work. It's the "aha moment" that demonstrates to potential clients why your agency's thinking is perfectly suited to solve their problems.

Don't skip this! This section is often overlooked, but it's

the most critical part of the case study. Readers want to see how you arrived at your solution, not just what you did. Peeking behind the curtain to understand your thought process is what sets your agency apart.

**PROSPECT-FRIENDLY ACTIONS**

**Mark Astone, CEO, Catalyst Marketing**

*"You have to show that you have done the homework. Show that you've got a pretty doggone good feel for the market, their brand, where they want to go with their brand, the other brands in the market, what the customers are feeling, so you can come in with something that's authentic. Provided you can do that, no one can compete with you."*

3. **Strategy:**

   Explain the strategy that directly stemmed from your key insight. Clearly define your target audiences, the methods you used to reach them, and why you believed your message would resonate with them at the right time and place.

4. **Execution:**

   Show how your insight-driven strategy translated into an efficient and effective plan. Provide clear context: how does each element of your execution (e.g., creative campaign, media plan) directly connect back to the core insight and strategy? Don't assume the connection is obvious! Explicitly explain how the pieces fit together to showcase the brilliance of your approach. You're already doing the work; now clearly demonstrate it.

5. **Results:**

   Outline all measurable results, including ongoing optimizations and key learnings. Crucially, demonstrate how these results directly address the initial challenge and objectives. Ensure alignment: if your objective was to increase sales, your results should showcase sales growth, not just social engagement.

Once you have all the elements, craft a compelling title that speaks directly to the case's core achievement (e.g., revenue boost, sales increase, brand awareness). Consider developing a creative theme to guide the overall narrative. For creative campaigns, integrate visual samples throughout the case study, rather than presenting them in a separate "creative dump." The most effective case studies weave creative elements into the fabric of the story, demonstrating how each piece was strategically designed to address a specific challenge. Show, don't just tell, how your creative work solved the problem.

By incorporating all five key elements, you'll create a clear and compelling case study that reads like a story, building expectation and delivering a satisfying payoff. Most importantly, it directly answers the prospect's critical question: "What can this agency do for my business?" If, however, any of these elements are missing, or if any section drags on, you risk losing your audience — and potentially missing your opportunity to shine. Don't let a weak case study dim your agency's potential.

**PROSPECT-FRIENDLY ACTIONS**

**Jenn Anhorn, retired VP, Business Development (Quad & Periscope)**

*"Case studies can take an unbelievable amount of time to customize for every single RFP or review. Having a repository of case resources to build from is mission-critical. Otherwise, you're always one step behind and you can't scale."*

The Brandon Agency's wonderful work is captured in a case study for FIREDISC Cookers, presented below, demonstrating the effectiveness of our recommended format.

---

## Cooking Up Greater Awareness and Sales for FIREDISC

### Challenge: Find New FIREDISC Cooks

FIREDISC Cookers initially set out to disrupt the outdoor cooking industry with an innovative portable propane cooker. They came to us with a challenge to increase their revenue and drive direct to consumer channel sales. With over 750 retailers and established DTC channels, FIREDISC Cookers had all the key elements to take the brand to the next level. However, the brand lacked awareness outside of the hunting, fishing, and camping markets. We needed to position the brand to expand appeal and drive sales, all on a modest budget.

*Objectives:*

- To lift all revenue, especially direct-to-consumer channel sales
- Increase awareness for FIREDISC products
- Increase preference for FIREDISC products

### Analysis: The Cooks are at Home

FIREDISC had a history of success as an outdoor enthusiast brand. They focused on the travel and portability of the product, which spoke to folks in that market. We needed to broaden the target.

FIREDISC had extensive research on the outdoor cooking and BBQ industry, but they hadn't used it to define new targets. The research told us that more people cook outdoors in their own backyards than they do hunting, fishing, or camping. To grow market share, we needed to reach people in their own backyard. We needed to target families. Luckily, the competition for backyard cooking was limited mainly to grills, none of which could compete with FIREDISC's cooking capabilities.

**Insight: Cooking Brings Families Together**

As the only outside cooker that offers a virtually indestructible seasoned cooking surface that is easy to clean, FIREDISC provided a quick and easy solution for families to cook outdoors. It made cooking simple. And because cooking is a traditional method of bringing people together, the FIREDISC gave families a chance to connect through the preparation and sharing of food. It created community.

The insight became clear: Simple Cooking + Community was the draw for FIREDISC. We called it "Fire It Up + Gather Round."

FIREDISC needed to show families that the product was perfect for their backyard and for family dinners. FIREDISC needed to become a backyard cooking staple.

**Strategy: Firing Up Families**

Our "Fire It Up + Gather Round" insight led us to a "Cooking + Community" focused strategy. We shifted resources to an aggressive emphasis on reaching families with family + food-centric imagery and content.

Budgets focused on leveraging more highly targeted messages to this newly defined audience. We showed up for families where they were — their social media consumption, their web activity, the channels they watch, and more. We wanted to connect with them and let them know that FIREDISC was a player in backyard cooking.

### What We Cooked Up

A key element of FIREDISC's success was an integrated marketing plan that was custom-tailored to their new target market.

- The family + food focus provided a brand-new feel for FIREDISC. We went through each channel and changed the messaging, creative, and visuals to focus on this new approach of "Fire It Up + Gather Round." The campaign required a substantial photo and video shoot showcasing families enjoying being together while cooking in their backyard. Everything came back to great food and making memories with family.
- For the website, we focused the content on the experience of great food and designed an easy-to-navigate site to help drive sales.
- We started from scratch with the media strategy, with moves such as shifting focus to chefs as influencers and establishing a presence on the Food Network instead of the Outdoor Channel.
- We also started a Facebook Live once a month to showcase cooking on the FIREDISC and to share recipes, where people now post pictures upon the arrival of their FIREDISC in the mail and request recipes.

### Results That Cook

The "Fire It Up + Gather Round" campaign achieved FIREDISC's objectives of growing revenue, awareness, and preference. As FIREDISC expanded its reach within this new audience, total website revenue increased by over 573% since November 2019. Additionally, revenue per user doubled, proving that the messaging, creative, and media strategy resonated with families, as well as the traditional market of outdoor enthusiasts.

- Website revenue has increased over 573%
- Revenue per user has increased 52%
- Amazon revenue has increased 480%
- Average order value has increased 110%
- Paid Social ROAS – 963%
- Paid Search ROAS – 248%

### A Few Thoughts About the FIREDISC Case

In the FIREDISC case study, note that the structure is built around the five elements we outlined, but with titles that add a bit of creative flair. Even if a reader doesn't have time to read the whole thing in depth, they can grasp, at a glance, the flow of the story. Here's a breakdown of why this format works so well in this example:

**Definition (called "Challenge" in the case above):** Find New FIREDISC Cooks – This title creatively highlights the overall objective of growing revenue and direct consumer sales, leaving the rest of the section to flesh out the details.

**Analysis:** The Cooks are at Home – The title and section that follows explain how the research uncovered exactly who the new audience was, and where they could be found.

**Insight:** Cooking Brings Families Together – The insight section outlines how and why, given the family target and a sturdy product that was easy to use, The Brandon Agency decided to focus on the backyard and the creative space where cooking and community aligned.

**Strategy:** Firing Up Families – This powerful insight fueled the agency's strategic approach, providing a clear roadmap for reaching the target audience.

**Execution:** What We Cooked Up – We get to see what was done, i.e., the output, but because we were given the context of what came before, by now we're hopefully thinking, "Of course that's what they did." In other words, we get to focus on enjoying the creative samples rather than questioning them.

**Results:** Results That Cook – The campaign delivered outstanding results, directly hitting targets for both awareness and revenue.

By framing the case in this format, we not only get a glimpse of the agency magic that went into building the insight and strategy (even with a product as decidedly unmagical as a backyard grill), we can also check off the expected standards: business issues, clear objectives, and demonstrable results. With this example, The Brandon Agency has built a truly prospect-centric case study that still highlights the agency's involvement.

For brevity, this version of the case study focuses on the written content. In a full presentation, this would be complemented by relevant visuals.

### Four Case Study Formats

We often get asked, "How long should a case study be?" Our answer: it depends. The key is to tell the right story for the right purpose. Here's a breakdown of four case study formats and their ideal use cases:

1. **Long Form**

   This is the most thorough case study, as we outlined above. It tells the complete story with complementary graphics. One long-form case study can be adapted for many different uses, such as a proposal, your agency website, or a video.

2. **Short Form**

   This tells the complete story in a slightly truncated manner, often with few graphics. It includes enough information to instill confidence in your strategic process, but does so by focusing on the sections of Challenge, Insight, Strategy, and Results. Sections dedicated to Research and Execution can be minimized or eliminated, as long as the others are still clearly tied together. This is appropriate for your agency website, as well as a proposal or presentation.

3. **Caselet**

   This is a mini case study that is often a summary of the full case study's story highlights told in only a couple of lines or points. It includes enough information to intrigue prospects and demonstrate past results. The focus is on the challenges your agency undertook for the client and the results created from your strategy. Like the other formats, this can be used on your website, and it's a great format to use for presentations and proposals, as it doesn't take up a lot of real estate in the pitch that isn't specifically focused on the prospect's needs.

4. **Droplet**

   A droplet is simply a one-sentence description highlighting past work that is relevant to the prospect. The droplet includes the brand you supported, the business challenge, the strategy or tactic the agency used, and the outcome. An example: "Our recommendation is similar to how we helped FIREDISC shift to a new family-focused target audience and increase ecommerce sales by +573%." These types of cases can be sprinkled into any conversation you have with a prospect, like a Q&A or a pitch, and they'll add weight to your words while letting you tout your successes in brief.

### An Underused Trick: The Droplet

In an agency proposal, the artful placement of a single, powerful sentence can be the difference between winning and losing.

And the perfect line added to your formal or informal pitch, in the right context, can add great weight to your agency's capabilities and the prospect's confidence in you and your team.

The droplet is your secret weapon: a perfectly crafted sentence that builds trust and wins you business.

The droplet confidently proclaims, "We've successfully tackled challenges like this before," and backs it up with compelling evidence.

To help you create effective droplets, we've developed a simple, fool-proof formula:

"Our (**work**) helped (**brand**) overcome (**challenge**) by (**strategy or tactic**) which resulted in (**result**)."

Ready to create your own droplets? This easy-to-use formula will guide you. Here's an example from our experience at Mercer Island Group:

"The **Mercer Island Group agency search process** helped **Ulta Beauty choose McCann** and McCann has helped the retailer **achieve record revenue and profitability since 2017."**

Droplets can be used in a variety of situations:

- Add one to a cover note after focusing mainly on the prospect
- Insert one into a written proposal when describing key capabilities
- Pepper your pitch presentations with an occasional droplet while talking about the prospect's business and challenges

In essence, a droplet can be sprinkled into virtually any discussion or interaction you're having with a prospect, from an informal chat to a Q&A or a pitch.

Droplets add weight to your words while letting you tout your successes briefly.

Refer to the visual below for a helpful reminder:

## DROPLETS

### THE SIMPLE FORMULA FOR BUILDING A DROPLET:

"Our (**insight/work/etc.**) helped (**brand**) overcome (**challenge**) by (**strategy or tactic**) which resulted in (**result**)."

### AN EXAMPLE OF A DROPLET:

**"Our recommended approach is similar to how we helped FIREDISC shift to a new family-focused target audience and increase ecommerce sales by +573%."**

### USAGE:

**Droplets can be sprinkled into any conversation you have with a prospect, like a Q&A or a pitch, and they'll add weights to your words while letting you tout your successes in brief."**

Droplets are perfect for a quick jolt of credibility. Much like the best ad copy, there is strength in brevity. Highlight only what's most compelling. Try them in your next written proposal or presentation!

### Where To Use Case Studies

Now that you're familiar with the different types of case studies, let's examine the best channels for sharing them and the specific considerations for each platform.

**Website** case studies should be concise but comprehensive enough to build confidence in your strategic process. Remember to showcase your insights, not just your research. Readers are more interested in how you achieved results than just what you did (but don't neglect the results!). Let your agency's thinking shine. Guide readers through your discovery process, connecting all the dots as you would in a client presentation. Prioritize usability. Make your case studies easily filterable and shareable for maximum convenience.

**Presentation** case studies must directly address the prospect's specific business issues at hand — the very reason they're seeking a new agency. Even if the connection seems obvious, explicitly explain why you chose this particular case study. Better yet, use the language from the RFP to demonstrate how this case aligns with their needs. Important note: Unless requested, we advise against dedicating entire slides to case studies in your pitch. Instead, weave case stories into your presentation to support your claims. This is the perfect place for the droplet format. In all cases, craft a compelling narrative, clearly linking the insight to the strategy to the execution, and keeping the story concise and relevant to the client's needs.

**Written proposal** case studies should be carefully customized to address challenges similar to those the prospect is facing. Emphasize areas (issues, targets, results, etc.) that directly align with the prospect's needs and trim any irrelevant sections. As with presentations, clearly explain the relevance of each case study and demonstrate how that experience has prepared you to effectively partner with the prospect. Show, don't just tell, how your past success translates to their future success.

## Even More Case Study Tips

Implement these strategies to ensure your case studies stand out from the competition:

1. **Explain Clearly Why You Selected the Case**

   Frame why the case is special and how the prospect should think about it.

   For example, if you are responding to an RFP and part of the "ask" was to share your agency's experience with helping a retailer in a highly competitive industry increase ecommerce sales, play that request right back at the reader at the beginning of the case:

   > *Retailer is a premium furniture brand, sells its modern products both nationally online and in regionally limited brick-and-mortar stores. Their ecommerce sales are underperforming. We've included this case study to highlight our Agency's proven experience with retail brands in highly competitive industries. It demonstrates our holistic approach to rapidly boosting ecommerce sales, a key challenge Retailer is currently facing.*

   Help your prospect appreciate your agency by telling them what to look for in a case!

**2. Include a "Quick Hits" Summary Upfront**

A sound approach is to quickly capture the reader's attention with a quick, easy-to-read summary upfront, including the great results. This is *in addition* to the longer case story.

> **CASE STUDY QUICK HITS**
>
> **Goal:** Turn around disappointing ecommerce trends.
>
> **Objective:** Grow annual ecommerce sales by +10% year over year.
>
> **Analysis:** Our analysis uncovered key learning about the client's ecommerce site: multiple design flaws (wayfinding, checkout, and SEO) resulting in traffic not converting
>
> **Site Enhancements:** In only 30 days, we redesigned site flow, fixed check out, and enhanced SEO
>
> **Results:** 12-month ecommerce revenue increased +14% year over year despite a 20% reduction in advertising

A strong summary immediately grabs the attention of busy "skimmers" while also enticing committed readers to explore the full case study.

**3. Use Storytelling Principles**

Make your cases "inviting to read." To create inviting and engaging case studies, focus on these key elements:

- An engaging title: Capture attention and convey the core message
- A consistent theme: Create a cohesive and memorable narrative
- Compelling visuals: Use visuals that enhance the story and showcase your work
- All the key chapters:
  *The challenge & objective*
  *Your analysis & insights*
  *The strategy*
  *Tactics (Execution)*
  *Results*

Don't let a weak case study dim your agency's potential.

**PROSPECT-FRIENDLY ACTIONS**

**Andie Jewett, SVP, Client Engagement, Team Lewis**

*"Case studies are crucial in the pitch process, but what's more crucial is how we storytell the case. Clients want to understand that we not only understand their industry, but we have experience solving similar business challenges. In fact, in some instances, we might show a case study that's outside the category because it perfectly encapsulates the client's needs. When we directly explain WHY we are presenting this particular work sample, the client feels like we listened, and we 'get' them."*

## 4. The Insight Is Key

Regardless of format or length, our core advice for creating effective case studies remains consistent: the power lies in the story and its presentation. For the longer formats, the insight is paramount. For the shorter forms (caselets and droplets), the strategy and results take center stage.

For the longer formats, be sure to include the insight.

- *A consistent theme: Create a cohesive and memorable narrative*
- *Compelling visuals: Use visuals that enhance the story and showcase your work*

If you can tie the whole story together (from challenge to results) with the insight as the linchpin, you have a truly intriguing case study. This is a case study that readers will be eager to read (and, we all hope, follow up on).

For the shorter formats, you want to make an impact with the agency strategy and results. Much like the best ad copy, there is strength in brevity. Highlight only what's most effective. If that changes (e.g., from higher social engagement to awareness lift) based on who you're talking to, it will be even better.

### Case studies aren't just tools for building new business.

Agencies often overlook a crucial opportunity to leverage case studies: expanding business with the existing client featured in the case. We strongly believe in organic growth, and strengthening existing client relationships is the most effective path. While pursuing new business is essential, don't miss the opportunity to demonstrate your value and grow your partnership with current clients. Showing them how you've solved similar problems for others can be incredibly persuasive.

Case studies are a highly effective tool to include at year-end meetings when asking for an expansion in scope, as they remind the client of the details of your previous year's work on their behalf. They also make a great pre-packaged story your client can share internally to showcase their (and, not incidentally, your) success over the previous year.

By sharing success with the client and putting the spotlight on them (either in a meeting or, more publicly, by including the case study on your website), you help your client look like a hero.

And that helps everyone involved.

---

### EXERCISE: CASE STUDY REVIEW

- Do your case studies have each key section?
- Do your case studies include a summary upfront?
- Do you have versions of each type of case study (Long Form, Short Form, Caselet, and Droplet)?

# CHAPTER 7
# Readiness Tools: The Prospect-Friendly Website

Is your agency website prospect-friendly?

It should go without saying (but we'll say it anyway), if you are serious about business development, you'd better be serious about your website. Outside of a personal recommendation, it's the single most important tool in your agency's toolkit.

Many potential buyers find their way to your website, and you have no idea they are there. Your website's core mission is to capture their attention and interest enough so that your agency can be considered.

How does a prospect end up on your page? It could be an internet search because of the need for a new agency. Perhaps someone recommended your work to a company owner, and they are curious. Maybe a news article sparked an interest in knowing more about what is going on in the agency world.

## Imagine This Scenario

A senior executive or owner of a company decides the firm needs a new agency and tasks a middle manager with identifying agencies providing the following specific criteria:

> *"We need a PR agency with retail experience — preferably in the kid's sector — to manage the campaign for our new Santa Fe location opening in January."*

The executive quickly lists these requirements:

- Public relations expertise
- Experience with kids' retail
- Proven store opening track record
- Familiarity with Santa Fe
- Located in our time zone
- No current work for our three main competitors

And that is it. The middle manager needs to create a list and make sure that the agencies on the list are a good fit vis-à-vis the brief spec list.

Additionally, this task is assigned alongside the middle manager's existing full-time responsibilities.

And remember when we said that they know very little about agencies? They don't read industry-specific publications like *Campaign*, *Ad Age*, *Adweek*, or *PR Week* with the same devotion as agency executives, and they're only vaguely familiar with the names of a couple of agencies. Asking friends and colleagues for advice may add one or two more names to the list — if they're lucky — but mostly they're left to figure it out on their own.

Their next step is to use a search engine or an AI tool to help broaden and extend their short list of candidate agencies.

And between their friends' advice, some search and AI investigation, and their own limited knowledge, they put together a list.

With the list in hand, they begin exploring the websites of the agencies they've shortlisted. If they're fortunate, they'll come across your website!

What visitors discover when they arrive at your website will likely determine whether your agency stays on their shortlist. They need quick, clear answers to their questions — especially since this task is in addition to their full-time job.

The most crucial information is whether your agency is the right fit for their company's needs. For example, if they're looking for a PR firm, can they immediately tell that public relations is your specialty? If it's not obvious right away, they'll probably move on to the next agency on their list.

From there, any number of easily locatable facts could lead them further into your website, such as:

- Is their company's industry represented in your agency's experience?
- Is your agency B2C or B2B?
- Does your agency do the kind of work they need done?
- How big is your agency?
- Who are your agency's current clients?
- Where does the agency have offices?

If they can't quickly validate or verify that you're relevant to their checklist, there's a good chance they will remove you from the list and move on. There are too many agencies to review for them to devote too much time exploring any one agency's website. You want to undercut any impulse they might have to move on with clear, helpful, engaging information.

It's important to imagine your website as one of the maps a prospect needs while on their buyer's journey. However they got here, they're on your website and you need them to stay and find what they need to know. The easier it is for them to check the right boxes for your agency, the greater the odds that you stay on the list.

Keep in mind, it's not about how YOU perceive your website. As an insider, everything might seem clear and intuitive to you. What truly matters, however, is that any prospect visiting your site can quickly and easily find and understand how to find all the essential information they need to make their decision.

Let's explore some key elements to help ensure that your website is the most powerful calling card that it can be.

## Elements of Prospect-Friendly Websites

While it's important to showcase your agency's creativity and accomplishments, it should never come at the cost of providing potential clients with what they truly want: fast and easy access to the information they need. No matter how successful your agency is, never assume everyone is already familiar with your name.

You're aiming to connect with clients and prospects who may not be deeply versed in the industry details or agency landscape. Your website must recognize and respect that reality.

So, if you view your website through the eyes of a potential client who knows little about agencies and needs quick, clear answers about who you are and what you offer, how approachable and straightforward does your site feel?

Everything that goes on your website should be put there with a prospect in mind. Your frame of reference is instantly clear, so the prospect looks for additional items on their spec list. Capabilities are shared so the prospect knows what you can do. Experience is shared so the prospect knows what you've done. Industry insights help establish you as an expert in a field that could benefit the prospect. When reviewing your website, ask yourself why each element is included. Every single answer needs to start with, "Because the prospect ..."

A prospect-friendly website has three key characteristics:

1. Clear agency positioning
2. Highly functional
3. Content rich

By successfully checking off these elements from the prospect's perspective, you help to create the momentum that could lead to a conversation with the potential to build more business for your agency.

How do these elements come to life on a prospect-friendly agency website?

**1. The Agency Is Clearly Positioned**

- **Frame of Reference**
  Does your homepage instantly communicate the type of work your agency does and the clients you serve? Prospects need to grasp exactly what you offer — and who it's for — within a second. If it's not clear, they'll likely move on.
- **Distinctive Positioning**
  The agency positioning statement you developed earlier in this book should be immediately evident from the homepage. Beyond that, your agency philosophy, strategic process, and interaction process should be naturally reflected throughout the entire website from the "Home" to "Case Studies" to "About Us."

**2. The Agency Website is Highly Functional**

- **Navigation**
  While a visually striking homepage is important, potential clients will quickly lose interest if they must search extensively for the information they need. Frustration sets in fast, and they may leave your site — and your services — behind.

- **Expected Content**
  Prospects expect to find certain standard industry sections that answer their key questions, such as:
  - Capabilities
  - Clients
  - Case studies
  - Staff bios
  - Awards
  - Contact information
  - Fact sheets
- **Search Functionality**
  Too many agency websites lack a strong search feature that allows visitors to quickly pinpoint what they're looking for. Always design your site with the potential client in mind — someone unfamiliar with your agency — and ensure your site is optimized for effective searching.

**3. Great User Experience**

- **User Friendly**
  All essential information should be easy to read, view, and understand at a glance.
- **Shareable**
  Wherever possible, content should be easy to share, enabling prospects to pass along helpful information and increase your agency's visibility.
- **Video**
  Use videos strategically to support and enhance your message, not as distracting "visual noise." Make sure videos load quickly; slow videos can give a negative impression of your agency.

- **Mobile Friendly**
  Your website must perform seamlessly across all devices, from small five-inch smartphone screens to large desktop monitors, providing a consistent and accessible experience.

## 4. Your Agency's Website is Content Rich

- **Capabilities**
  Present your agency's capabilities clearly and concisely using standard industry terminology. Avoid inventive, creative new names for services — while it may seem inventive, it often confuses prospects. For example, if you buy media, simply state that rather than calling yourself an "audience connector." While differentiating your agency is important, clarity here is essential for immediate understanding.

- **Experience**
  When showcasing your past experience, focus on addressing a potential client's key questions rather than just highlighting vanity metrics. Organize your experience so it's easy to navigate through one of these methods:

  1. Sortable by Industry (e.g., Financial, Retail, Hospitality)
  2. Sortable by Medium (e.g., Branding, Media, Public Relations)
  3. Sortable by both Industry and Medium

- **Case Studies & Work Samples**
  Case studies should clearly outline the challenge, analysis and insights, strategy, tactics, and results. Work samples should include the objectives and measurable outcomes to provide context and impact.

- **Bios**
  Your team section should emphasize the experience and successes of key members, accompanied by professional photos that complement your agency's brand personality. Highlight relevant credentials such as prominent clients, industry expertise, individual awards, years of experience, and previous agency roles. Share details that build confidence in your team.

- **News & Awards**
  Keep this section current with industry recognition, accolades, and media mentions to demonstrate ongoing credibility and success.

- **Contact Us**
  List all office locations clearly, marking the main office prominently along with direct phone numbers to reach you. Avoid relying solely on generic contact forms, which can be off-putting. Also, include information about current job openings to attract prospective employees.

- **Thought Leadership**
  Showcase newsletters, published books, or articles by agency team members, e-books, or a company blog that shines a spotlight on your agency's expertise in business challenges, industries, or processes. This reinforces your position as a knowledgeable leader in the field.

- **Fact Sheet**
  Offer a downloadable fact sheet containing key data such as office locations, number of employees, client types, and core capabilities. This is especially valuable for mid-level managers tasked with researching agencies and presenting findings to senior decision-makers, often those who ultimately make the final choice.

An agency's website is its storefront to the world. Prospects will visit and browse without you knowing they are there, so it is important that they can find what they need quickly and effectively.

---

## EXERCISE: REVIEW YOUR WEBSITE

We've developed a checklist in the Appendix that agencies can use to evaluate their websites against Mercer Island Group's best practices, with each item assigned a numeric value for a total of 100 possible points. Use this tool to assess your site's ease of use and the key elements included, giving you a clear picture of your website's current performance. In our experience, most agency websites score between 40 and 60 points. Setting a target of 80 or higher is recommended, with ongoing plans for improvement.

# CHAPTER 8
# Readiness Tools: The Five Slides

Throughout this book, we've emphasized time and again the importance of putting the prospect first and focusing less on yourself and your agency. That core message will carry through to the very last page. But now, it's time for a little self-promotion — with a twist. The key is to view your self-promotion from the prospect's perspective.

Yes, even when you're talking about yourself, your goal should always be to prioritize the client.

**It's never about you ... even when it is.**

We often see that when agencies get a chance to present to a prospect, the presentation begins with slide after slide about the agency itself. Usually, it's disconnected and lacks a clear story because the agency puts it together without really considering what will be interesting or relevant to the client. This often leads to 5, 10, or even 15 minutes of self-promotion before finally shifting focus to the prospect, where it should have been all along.

Yes, you need to showcase your agency, but simply talking about yourself isn't the right approach. As we've emphasized before, you bond with prospects over their problem, not your solution.

There's a better way. Never start by talking about yourself!

Instead, engage the potential client by showcasing how much you understand about their company and their objectives. There's a time to remind the prospect of why you are the best agency for the partnership, but that time fits better later in the arc of your pitch.

In our experience, the right time to talk about the agency is after you've shared your understanding of the client's challenge and recommended strategy, but before you present your proposed tactics. This is the ideal way to demonstrate how your agency can bring value to the solution.

And the way to introduce the prospect to the agency is with five special slides.

Not six slides. Not seven slides. It's just FIVE SLIDES.

Our experience has shown that five slides are the perfect number to showcase an agency's strengths, experience, and expertise. Just five. The rest of the presentation should be focused on explaining how you would address and solve the prospect's business challenges.

Frequently, while working with agencies through this exercise, they have come to us to say, "We have seven slides about us because there's some important stuff we need to include. Is that okay?" And there has yet to be a time when the response has been, "Yeah, that's worth seven slides."

Five slides. No more. No less.

## THE FIVE SLIDES

These five slides represent the essential windows into everything about your agency. If someone is interested, they'll ask a question. If not, you've shared just enough information about your credentials to inform anyone unfamiliar with your firm.

The first three slides are based on the positioning statement you developed earlier in this book:

### Slide 1: Philosophy

The slide highlights what is special about your agency, shaping how clients should perceive your firm.

### Slide 2: Strategic Process

Here, you outline the step-by-step process you use to solve client problems. It demonstrates that you have a proven, repeatable method for uncovering insights that lead to success, showing your approach is deliberate and dependable, not just luck.

### Slide 3: Interaction Philosophy

This slide explains what it's like to work with your agency, setting expectations for collaboration and communication.

### Slide 4: Capabilities

A brief overview of your agency's capabilities helps the prospect understand how many ways you can support their needs, often revealing additional services they weren't aware of. Clients frequently come back and say, "Oh, you do that too?"

### Slide 5: Logos

The final slide displays logos of current or past clients that are relevant to the prospect. These can be clients from the same industry, or clients that had the same business challenge. Or possibly clients with similar scale or geographic coverage. Impressive client brand names help. This slide's goal is to work as a risk reducer, allowing the prospect to think, "If those guys hired this agency, maybe we should, too."

The point is simple: showcase logos that will help the prospect feel comfortable that your agency has relevant experience that will benefit them.

### Other Slides

That's it. You don't need a slide dedicated to your awards or your agency's history. When it comes to the pitch, prospects aren't concerned with how long you've been in business — they care whether you understand their challenges and can help them solve them.

These five slides together create a complete, relevant picture of the agency for the prospect. When building a pitch deck, your focus should be entirely on the prospect's company, needs, and challenges. You shouldn't be building these slides from scratch each time, and many of them are easy to reuse:

- The Philosophy, Strategic Process, and Interaction Process slides generally stay the same.
- The Capabilities slide can be customized to highlight the specific services most relevant to the prospect.
- The Logo slide is often tailored to include relevant client logos for that particular opportunity, making it as impactful and relevant as possible.

Minimizing the amount of time you talk about your agency maximizes your potential to impress the client. It indicates that you are comfortable enough and confident enough to let your work, insight, and empathy for the prospect's business needs speak for itself.

The Five Slides are concise and focused, allowing you to dedicate most of your time to connecting with and understanding your prospect.

---

## EXERCISE: THE FIVE SLIDES

Take a look at your most recent pitch presentation:

- How many slides focused on the agency?
- Were the logo and capabilities slides customized to suit the prospect?
- Does your agency have the Five Slides ready to use on a moment's notice?

# CHAPTER 9
# Readiness Tools: The Prospect-Friendly Response Template

The ideal agency presentation looks like it was handcrafted specifically for the audience. You want the prospect to see themselves in your presentation.

The art here is to have an easy-to-populate template that enables a sense of co-branding: your agency's brand and the prospect's brand, look and feel.

The goal is to have a template that the prospect still views as being customized for their company and brand. A sound template enables you to easily and quickly enhance the appearance of customization with images of the prospect's logos, storefronts, industries, or target audience. These steps enable your agency to easily create the (appropriate) impression that their company is your focus and that, if they hire you, they'll be treated as if they're the only client you have.

## Prospect-Friendly Response Template Basics

**Slide Template:** Your slide template should have both agency branding and an easy-to-populate area for the prospect's logo.

There are also a handful of slides that can be established to include a space or slot to add the prospect's imagery. Cover slides, section slides, and section dividers are all examples of this kind of slide.

**Prepackaged Content with Limited Customization:** Many basic content slides can be prepopulated with basic content and include sections for additional customization. Capabilities are a good example. A capabilities section can be ready to go with basic content, leaving open slots for customization, such as adding special caselets or client logo examples.

**Prepack the Five Slides:** Your agency philosophy, process, and interaction philosophy slides can be ready to go. These do not need customization. The capabilities slide should be prepackaged with an ability for easy editing, enabling appropriate tailoring on the go. The logo slide should be predesigned, with easy access to a library of logos organized by industry and business challenge.

**The Beauty:** While it may seem like common sense, our experience tells us that we should also highlight the importance of making sure the look and feel of your deck is appealing. Prospects expect agencies to be masters of beautiful and compelling communications.

**The Evidence:** It's beneficial to have specific examples of past work organized in advance for easy access. For instance, you might have one set of samples and case studies organized by industry, medium, and business challenge.

# CHAPTER 10
# You're Invited to Pitch - What's Next?

Your hard work has paid off — positioning finalized, website prospect-ready, marketing in motion, and your network built. Now an opportunity surfaced!

It may be a warm lead, an inbound inquiry, or even a formal RFP.

No matter where the lead comes from, there are immediate actions you should take to determine whether this opportunity is worth pursuing.

You probably have a lot of questions: *What do we REALLY know about this company? What do they actually need? Are we the right agency for them? How should we interpret their RFP to shape the best approach?*

Without a clear plan to answer those questions, deciding whether to pursue the opportunity can quickly become stressful.

## Evaluating the Opportunity

*Before committing to a pitch, follow these three key steps:*

1. Build a business profile of the prospect
2. Ask targeted, clarifying questions
3. Qualify the opportunity against your agency's fit and priorities

## 1. Create a Business Profile

Job one is to prepare yourself for the important steps and decisions ahead. Start with some quick homework. Doing your homework allows you to better understand the prospect's business, industry, and potential business issues as you evaluate the opportunity. Not doing your homework is like playing the lottery with your new business approach; someone occasionally wins, but often, you walk away empty-handed.

Luckily, there is a quick, efficient, and proven process that can help you quickly come up to speed on the prospect's business: create a business profile. A business profile provides a structured overview of a prospect's company, including their potential challenges and opportunities where you can add the most value.

Many agencies only scratch the surface with their research, sticking to simple stats or a brief review of current news. A better alternative is to create a business profile that paints an entire picture of the prospect's business. By reviewing all aspects of a business, your firm will be better positioned to uncover the right information and to identify the core business issues for a prospect (positive and negative).

In addition to identifying key issues for your prospects, the standard practice of creating a business profile for each new potential client comes with the following advantages:

- Goes beyond marketing to identify the key business issues driving client and marketing decisions
- Provides a systematic approach and expectations across team members
- Trains junior team members on research best practices
- Prepares you to best position your solutions

A business profile should capture all relevant information about the prospect. The list below outlines the types of data to collect — it's comprehensive and requires time and resources, but this is essential to move you closer to winning the pitch.

### Business Profile Elements

What should be included in a business profile, and where can you find this information?

A comprehensive business profile typically covers the following sections:

- Company overview
- Company culture
- Channel highlights
- Business or retail calendar and seasonality
- Products and services
- Customer base
- Online presence
- Financial data
- Employee headcount
- Number of locations
- Marketing partners
- Media spend
- Industry classification
- Competitors
- New products and company news
- Corporate headquarters
- Key executives

Most of the information is readily available. Some key sources include:

- Special AI tools developed for agencies like Waldo.fyi
- General AI tools like ChatGPT, Perplexity, and others
- Analyst reports
- Trade associations
- The prospect's corporate website

After gathering all this information, compile it into a concise document that highlights the key data. This profile will guide your questions and serve as a foundation for your pitch preparation. Creating a well-informed business profile offers several advantages that can significantly boost your chances of success:

- It enables you to connect with clients through meaningful conversations about their business challenges, rather than delivering a one-sided presentation of your services.
- It positions you as a valuable business partner by allowing you to tailor your solutions to directly address their specific issues.
- It enhances your credibility, making your questions and pitch feel more personalized and relevant to the prospect, rather than relying solely on past work or case studies.
- It demonstrates your understanding of their business and your ability to add value — even if initial tactical ideas don't fully hit the mark.

Just one of the many benefits of putting together this profile is to gain a clear understanding of how the prospect talks about themselves and their business, enabling you to use prospect-friendly language in your discussions and potential pitch.

Want to connect more effectively with your agency's prospects? Speak their language, not yours.

If they have a revenue challenge, call it a revenue challenge. Not a sales challenge. If they have a sales challenge, call it a sales challenge. Not revenue or growth. Many of the words may generally mean about the same thing... but language has nuance and there is no point in taking such a risk.

To demonstrate the power of language in building connections with your prospects, let's begin with a quick story about Pet Parents. That's right – Pet Parents.

**Pet Parents**

What should be included in a business profile, and where can you find this information?

A few years ago we ran a pitch for a leading retail pet store.

Interestingly, the team at the pet store never calls their target audience "pet owners." Instead, they always refer to them as "pet parents." They genuinely LOVE pets, and this passion is deeply embedded in their culture.

This use of "pet parents" was clearly reflected throughout all of the briefing materials.

Moreover, the client team consistently used this terminology during the Q&A sessions.

Despite all of this, one of the finest agencies in the world approached the pitch in such an arrogant fashion that they missed this critical point. Instead of using the prospect's "pet parents" language, they instead continuously referred to their audience as... pet owners.

But wait, it gets better...

As the agency continued their presentation, they introduced signage ideas for different sections of the client's stores. There was signage for dogs, cats, and fish. Signs for pet food and accessories.

And then things went completely off the rails with their signage idea for the large lizard section:

*"Pets that eat other pets."*

They believed they were clever, but our client was deeply upset.

A pet parent doesn't talk that way about pets.

As you might expect that agency did not come out on top.

Or, to quote the CEO at the time: "Who the f—k invited that agency?"

Knowing and respecting a prospect's language and culture can go a long way to instilling confidence and rapport with a potential client. Missing these important queues is a good way to lose the opportunity.

## 2. Ask Questions

The business profile and initial conversations should give you a solid understanding of the prospect's situation. There will likely be, however, some key questions that remain unanswered. Before submitting your formal response, it's crucial to clarify these points. We've often been surprised by how few agencies ask for clarification or further details related to the RFP or request.

**PROSPECT-FRIENDLY ACTIONS**

**Brad Casper, CEO, Heart & Soul**

*"Before an agency can set themselves apart with their copywriting or creative development, they must first demonstrate to prospective clients and agency search consultants they can also master the art of asking the right questions. The right discovery questions are like a GPS to bring the agency to the right destination in the least amount of time. These questions are your initial showcase for how strategic and insightful of a partner you will be."*

When you first receive the RFP or request, don't hesitate to ask questions before committing to participate. Schedule a call if possible. Prepare questions that will help you assess whether this opportunity aligns with your agency's strengths and goals.

Some initial questions to consider include:

- Why are they conducting this review? Why now?
- Is there an incumbent agency, and are they involved in the process?
- What impact do they expect from the new agency on their business?

On average, only about three out of 10 agencies ask questions. It's rare to see the other seven agencies fully equipped with the necessary information!

Remember, you're 100% more likely to get an answer to a question you ask than one you don't ask. The worst-case scenario is that the prospect may respond with "Sorry, we're not taking any questions." Even that gives you valuable information about how they operate and can influence your decision about whether to move forward. Are you comfortable working with a client who won't communicate or clarify along the way?

**PROSPECT-FRIENDLY ACTIONS**

**Jenn Anhorn, retired VP, Development, Quad & Periscope**

*"You have to peel away a lot of layers of the onion to get to what is going to be the winning formula. It's hard to project out of the gate, but once you get the conversation going and you ask questions and you get more clarity and you can ask more questions, you can start to then reveal what's going to win this for us. But unless you can have that dialogue, you just can't. You're guessing."*

### 3. Qualify an Opportunity

For many agencies, the concept of turning down business is nearly impossible to grasp. Regardless of the agency's bandwidth of available resources, it's difficult to say no to any opportunity that comes along. But it's important to walk away from business when enough red flags indicate that it will be incredibly burdensome to say yes. Sometimes, these reasons fall on the agency side, such as when an agency is already committed to other pitches or onboarding new clients.

**PROSPECT-FRIENDLY ACTIONS**

**Clifton Alexander, Owner, Reactor**

*"The first thing we always do is we try to evaluate whether it's a good fit for us or not. Does this pitch fit with our strengths? Is this something that sits in our wheelhouse? Can we really talk confidently about this type of thing that they're asking us to do? How would we go about putting together a scope of work and a budget? And is it worth going all in, developing strategic insights, and doing some creative or a sample hype video? And how are we going to handle that from a timing perspective? And what's our workload look like? All that stuff obviously becomes a big factor in how we can handle it."*

Filters are critical to a healthy business development operation. Develop a list of defined new business filters that can help your agency quickly evaluate opportunities as they arrive. This helps the agency develop a shared point of view about the kinds of opportunities worth pursuing and the ones to pass.

Business development screening criteria often include:

- Project work vs. AOR
- Client budget
- Geography (national, regional, local)
- Company size
- Type of industry
- Type of business challenge
- Capabilities necessary
- Reputation of prospect
- Number of agencies invited to pitch

Before pitching a new client, evaluate the opportunity carefully and conduct your own research to determine if the effort and expense are justified.

The most important practical questions to consider are:

- How genuinely interested are you in the prospect?
- Is the potential return worth the investment and potential distraction, considering the size of the opportunity?

## Confirm Participation

You've asked the right questions, assessed the opportunity, and determined that you're genuinely interested and equipped to proceed. Now it's time to confirm participation with confidence and enthusiasm.

## EXERCISE: WHAT TO DO WHEN INVITED TO PITCH

- Does your agency create a business profile to guide how you approach and interact with prospects?
- What are your agency's criteria for new business opportunities? Are these filters effective? Are they consistently applied?

# CHAPTER 11
# Prospect-Friendly Pitch Planning

Having confirmed your participation in a competitive pitch or process, it's time to develop a plan for success.

## The Prospect-Friendly Pitch Plan

Delivering a compelling proposal or pitch is one of the most crucial skills an agency can develop to win new business. Achieving this requires thorough preparation and can be a significant investment — both financially and emotionally.

It's helpful to have a plan!

Once the pitch is scheduled, it's time to develop a winning strategy. The details of this plan will vary depending on whether the pitch is written, in person, or virtual. We've dedicated upcoming chapters to helping your agency deliver a powerful pitch, no matter the format.

Your prospect-friendly pitch preparation should include the following elements:

1. Pitch Calendar
2. Reengineered RFP (Request for Proposal)
3. Q&A Strategy
4. Identification of Potential Business Issues
5. Original Research

Each of these pieces works together to create a solid basis for your pitch and to ensure your team is on the road to success.

## PROSPECT-FRIENDLY ACTIONS

**Clifton Alexander, Owner, Reactor**

*"It is super important for me to sit with my whole team from the very beginning of an RFP process because then I can get them really excited about who the client is and what the scope of work is, and the fact that we've decided to go after this project and try to win it. If I can get the whole team really rallied around that, then I found that they will literally do just about anything that's required to make it happen."*

# CHAPTER 12
# Pitch Planning: The Pitch Calendar

Just as you wouldn't undertake an important client project without a timeline, why do many agencies participate in pitches without one? Successful pitch management depends on solid project management skills and planning.

A good pitch timeline becomes your roadmap to a more successful pitch.

A pitch timeline identifies the timing, steps, milestones, and responsibilities necessary to prepare a response that puts the agency's best foot forward. The pitch timeline will vary based on the timing, complexity, and asks for each pitch; however, most will cover important building blocks of a good pitch, including:

- RFP receipt and dissection
- Planning for and evaluating Q&A
- Preparation of a business profile
- Analysis of business issues
- Secondary and primary research planning and execution
- Strategic insight identification and strategy development
- Creative, media, and other solutions
- RFP drafting and finalization
- Rehearsal
- RFP submission and/or presentation

A straightforward approach to the pitch timeline is to structure it chronologically, counting down to the final deliverable. Appendix 4 in this book includes a sample for a 21-day pitch process.

Of course, you won't always have 21 days to prepare for a pitch. The example provided is simply meant to demonstrate how the process can be organized and adapted to suit your actual timeline. Remember, certain materials, such as case studies, can and should be prepared ahead of time and then tailored as necessary throughout the RFP process.

### PROSPECT-FRIENDLY ACTIONS

**Neil Smith, CMO, Crossmedia**

*"After running a few hundred pitches, the wins come from being highly organized, following a detailed timeline, and leaving proper time for design and rehearsal. Actors don't run onto the stage unless they're in costume, lines learned, and direction applied. Agencies shouldn't either. A winning pitch takes the right people doing the right things in the right order. Only with a detailed master timeline do you stand a chance of managing it all, and getting it done with enough time to polish and rehearse."*

## EXERCISE: PITCH CALENDARS

- Does your agency create a pitch calendar to guide each important pitch?
- Does your team consistently adhere to the calendar?
- Are there any areas where your agency tends to start later than ideal in the process?
- Looking back, what past mistakes could have been avoided if your team had consistently created and followed a detailed pitch calendar for each major opportunity?

# CHAPTER 13
# Pitch Planning: Reengineer the RFP

Reengineering the RFP process begins with a crucial step: reading the entire RFP thoroughly. While that may seem obvious, many of us tend to skim for what we see as the most important details and overlook the "fluff" in between.

Our recommendation is to read the RFP carefully in its entirety. Think of it like eating Oreos — you wouldn't skip the filling, as that's what makes it special. Similarly, fully understanding the full scope of the RFP requires engaging with every word to truly grasp the full picture.

Every. Single. Word.

And don't forget to read the cover letter. It's equally important and is oftentimes overlooked, which is a bit like tossing aside the card attached to a gift to tear off the paper to reach your new toy, completely missing that grandma slipped a twenty-dollar bill in the card. There's often value to be found in the cover letter.

A practical tip is to print out the RFI or RFP, along with the cover letter, and review it with a highlighter in hand. Highlight or circle key issues, important words, and relevant context as you go. Look for recurring patterns or themes. While it may be old-fashioned, this method remains highly effective. If you prefer digital, annotate your digital copy instead.

And, as you begin to dissect the request, consider every conversation you've had with or about this prospect. Take another look at your notes. What did you learn that can help identify business issues and implications?

What are their business challenges? What are the capabilities that they told us they need? What experiences do they think are relevant? What are potential conflicts? What do we know about their culture and what they might be looking for in the culture of an agency? These things are often easy to figure out if you have conversations or if you read carefully and allow yourself to see things through the client's eyes.

Look for recurring themes in what gets mentioned. Do they mention media buying a lot? Transparency? ROI?

These clues help you create a clearer picture of what the prospect might be looking for.

Try this exercise: review the sample RFP cover letter below and identify 10 key points that would assist in crafting an effective RFP response.

### Sample RFP Cover Letter

As you know, we are facilitating a confidential media agency review for Slip-ons Footwear.

Slip-ons' mission is to inspire everyone to lead healthier lifestyles by designing innovative gear that helps active individuals stay healthier and happier. This mission is embodied by Slip-ons' Walk Everywhere philosophy, a commitment to celebrating and promoting active living. The Slip-ons team and partners are energetic, outgoing, optimistic, and friendly. Paid media plays a vital role in how Slip-ons Footwear reaches its audience, and the company is seeking a strong strategic and tactical paid media agency partner. Location is not a limiting factor.

Slip-ons' growth has stalled, and the company is missing its financial targets amid several challenges. New competitors have entered the active footwear space, while established competitors have ramped up their marketing efforts in response. Meanwhile, Slip-ons' budgets have remained flat, and high inflation, coupled with an uneven economy, has negatively affected perception of the brand's pricing.

To recapture revenue and achieve their +5% target in units and sales, Slip-ons needs a strategic media partner capable of delivering impactful omnichannel campaigns. The ideal agency should have experience in footwear and active lifestyle categories, with proven capabilities in both brand (linear TV, CTV, video) and performance media (search, digital). They should also excel in holistic measurement and reporting. The U.S. media spend is approximately $30 million.

Slip-ons is seeking a strategic partner to develop a high-level plan outlining how to optimize the $30 million media budget to reach the revenue and unit growth goals. The plan should include audience targeting rationale, media channel recommendations that punch above their weight, and how these strategies align with the brand's Walk Everywhere philosophy and active lifestyle mission.

Please prepare your response according to the accompanying timeline.

---

What did you take away from this cover note?

Take a moment and jot down some notes.

Here are the key points we derived from the cover note:

- New competitors have entered Slip-ons' niche
- Established competitors are increasing marketing investments
- Inflation has diminished the brand's price perception

- The company is missing its financial goals
- Units and revenue have plateaued
- The goal is +5% growth in revenue and units
- The U.S. media budget is around $30 million
- The brand embraces a "Walk Everywhere" philosophy
- The ideal agency has omnichannel capabilities across brand and performance media
- Measurement and reporting are critical
- Both strategy and tactical execution are essential
- Experience in footwear and active lifestyle brands is preferable
- The client expects a media plan that can achieve its growth goals

These points offer clear guidance on Slip-ons' current situation and help shape a prospect-centric proposal.

With these notes in mind, it's time to craft a concise, one-page needs assessment summarizing the prospect's challenges and what they seek in an agency.

| NEEDS ASSESSMENT | |
|---|---|
| (a brief paragraph that identifies the prospect's situation, business challenges, goals, and needs in an agency) | |
| **Track Record & Expertise** | **Capabilities** |
| (the experiences and expertise that are critical for the agency to be the right agency; this can include case studies or spec proposals) | (the capabilities that are essential for the agency to succeed as well as nice-to-have capabilities) |
| **Size, Location & Culture** | **Assignment** |
| (the ideal agency size, location, and culture) | (key culture characteristics) |

Here's how you might draft a needs assessment using the notes from the cover letter (in actual practice, you would review and markup the entire RFP package!):

## NEEDS ASSESSMENT

Slip-ons sells casual footwear and apparel supporting its purpose to inspire everyone to be as active as possible. This purpose is expressed by Slip-ons' Walk Everywhere philosophy, a quest to celebrate and champion active lives. Increased competitive marketing investments, new competitors, and a challenging inflationary economy have stalled Slip-ons growth (flat units and revenue). Paid media is critical to Slip-ons marketing, and the company needs a strong strategic and tactical agency partner to turn around a flat business and drive +5% revenue and unit growth. The paid media budget is approximately $30 million. Unfortunately, the current agency has not been providing the necessary strategic leadership needed to help turn around the business. The ideal agency can help produce results across brand and performance, helping achieve the company's growth ambitions.

### Track Record & Expertise

**Client Experience**

- Footwear
- Active lifestyle brands

**Expertise**

- Strategic leadership
- Media planning that helps brands punch above their weight
- Brand and performance media

### Capabilities

**Strategy**

- Audience selection
- Holistic media strategy & planning
- Channel selection

**Media Activation**

- Brand media (linear TV, CTV, video)
- Performance media (search, digital)
- Measurement, analytics, modeling (MMM, MTA), reporting, optimization

### Size, Location & Culture

**Location:** Not important

**Culture:** active, outgoing, optimistic and friendly

### Assignment

A strategy and high-level plan regarding how Slip-ons should use its $30 million media budget to achieve +5% revenue and unit growth. Include your rationale regarding audience selection and media channels that can punch above their weight and deliver on the brand's goals.

After drafting the needs assessment, the final step is to estimate how the prospect might prioritize each aspect of your response. Occasionally, they will include grading criteria with the RFP, but more often than not, they won't. In those cases, you'll need to use your judgment to determine where to focus the majority of your effort and emphasis. This step is crucial in developing a prospect-friendly proposal that concentrates on what truly matters to the client.

Here's an example of how a grading criteria might be determined.

| SCORING CATEGORY | POTENTIAL POINTS |
|---|---|
| **Proposed Solution** | **50** |
| A strategy and plan Slip-ons could use with the $30 million media budget to achieve +5% revenue & unit growth. | 30 |
| Rationale regarding audience selection and media channels that can punch above their weight and deliver on the brand's goals. | 20 |
| **Evidence of Key Capabilities** | **40** |
| Media strategy (audience selection, media, & channel planning) | 20 |
| Activation (brand/performance media buying & measurement) | 20 |
| **Experience & Culture** | **10** |
| Experience (footwear and active lifestyle brands) and culture (active, outgoing, optimistic, and friendly) | 10 |
| **Total Points** | **100** |

## EXERCISE: REENGINEERING THE RFP

- How do you approach assessment of an RFP?
- What have you learned about evaluating RFPs?
- Do you create a needs assessment document as a summary of the client's needs?

# CHAPTER 14
# Pitch Planning: The Q&A

Good preparation is the foundation of every great pitch, and asking good questions is an important aspect of this process. In the last chapter, we talked about asking the right questions to ensure that the prospective business is worth pursuing. Those questions were about making sure the prospect is right for you.

Q&A questions serve a different purpose — they are designed to deepen your understanding of the prospect's business, marketing challenges, and needs. By asking thought-provoking questions, you can position your agency as the ideal partner, even before proposing solutions.

The objectives for a productive Q&A session should include:

- Building credibility by asking intelligent questions that demonstrate your knowledge of their business, industry, competition, target audience, and more.
- Gathering valuable information that can help craft a compelling and tailored proposal.

Whether conducted formally or informally, the Q&A process allows your agency to make a strong first impression through purposeful, thoughtful, and professional interactions. What you ask, and how you ask it, provides the prospect with a look into your strategic thinking, industry knowledge, and understanding of their company.

Additionally, the Q&A session is an essential opportunity to collect critical information for your response development.

To start, assign a dedicated Q&A coordinator responsible for formulating the right questions and orchestrating the call.

Next, prepare by doing your homework.

- Review of all provided materials (RFP, cover letter, brand book, etc.)
- Conduct your own research and review secondary sources
- Develop (or review) a detailed business profile
- Identify potential business issues the prospect might be facing

Focus your homework to uncover information that can help you frame the right Q&A questions:

- Consumer/customer needs
- Competitive situation
- Channels used by the prospect
- Brand/company situation
- Industry situation
- Business challenges and issues as represented in the RFP

Involve your pitch team. Gather questions from every pitch team member, organizing and prioritizing the questions most crucial to their business and your response. Your primary mission is to ask questions that can identify, prioritize, and add depth to your understanding of the prospect's business issues and corresponding implications (why the business issues matter).

For public companies, listen to the latest quarterly earnings call prior to the Q&A. Ask a question, if possible, while referring to the earnings call.

While questions will vary depending on the client and opportunity, here are some sample questions to help guide your thinking:

- Why are you searching for an agency now?
- What's going well for your business or brand, and what areas could be improved?
- What metrics does your company use to measure success (e.g., sales, revenue, profit)?
- How do you evaluate the success of your marketing efforts? What key metrics do you track?
- If not specified in the RFP, how do you define your core target audiences? Have those audiences changed over time? Do you have any research you can share about them?
- Which competitors are currently experiencing the most success and why?
- One year from now, after choosing an agency, what improvements or changes would you like to see?

Good questions can lead to a rich conversation that can easily fill the entire time of the Q&A session. Hold off on asking process questions that can easily be answered by email (i.e., timing, format, etc.). Process questions will not impress your prospect.

Before the Call: Once you have your list of questions finalized, share them with the prospect at least 24 hours in advance. This gives them time to research potential answers and ensure the right people will be on the call.

Also send along bios (with photos) of the agency team members that will be on the call. This small touch of professionalism is impressive and helps the prospect better relate to the agency folks involved.

During the call: Make sure your team has a single moderator (preferably, the proposed account lead). The moderator doesn't need to ask all the questions. Instead, it is her/his job to provide order by letting everyone know who will be asking questions, who from the agency side will answer client questions, and keep the call on time.

Begin the call with brief introductions: have each team member share their name and their role within the agency, and what role they will play on the business if the agency is selected.

After the call: Once you wrap up your call, follow up quickly with a note that:

- Thanks the prospect for their time and input
- Expresses enthusiasm for their business
- Recaps any outstanding questions or information the prospect promised as a follow up

Sometimes, Q&A is conducted solely in writing. If that's the case, be sure to:

- Be clear and concise in your responses
- Proofread your submission carefully
- Follow the same guidance as earlier about investigating key areas

Written Q&A responses are often shared with all participating agencies. If this happens, applying a disciplined and thorough approach will benefit you equally. We've heard agency executives hesitate to ask certain questions, fearing their competitors might see the responses. This is, however, counterproductive. If a question is important, ask it — your team can only benefit from the information. Don't worry about your competition and how they might use the responses.

*Additional tips include:*

- Ask questions that aren't easily answered through secondary research, such as information on the client's brand advantages/disadvantages, industry trends, or what marketing strategies have been successful or not.
- Request access to recent research or analyses the client might have.
- Avoid discussing your capabilities or past successes during this phase; focus on understanding the client.
- Assign clear roles within your pitch team — typically, leadership should handle opening and closing the session.
- Keep your questions brief and strategic; invest appropriate prep time to ensure clarity.
- Know when to end the Q&A — don't let it go on too long.
- If time is limited, ask something like, "Who would like to ask the last question?" to naturally manage the conversation.
- Seek permission to record the session; if recording isn't allowed, designate a note-taker to capture detailed notes.

Remember, Q&A isn't just about gathering information — it's also about building a strong relationship with the prospective client. It's a valuable opportunity to connect, establish trust, and lay the foundation for a successful partnership.

## EXERCISE: Q&A CALLS

- Does your agency have a documented approach to Q&A calls?
- Do you send your questions to the prospect in advance of the call?
- Are your Q&A calls planned with specific team roles?

# CHAPTER 15
# Pitch Planning: Determine Business Issues

The key to building rapport with prospects is to truly understand their challenges or opportunities.

We refer to these as "business issues" — the core problems or opportunities a business is aiming to address.

By leveraging the business profile, reengineered RFP, Q&A responses, and the research you've conducted, you should now be able to identify the specific business issues the prospect is facing. There are many potential challenges they might be seeking to resolve, including areas such as:

- *Revenue*
- *Profitability*
- *Customer acquisition*
- *Cost per acquisition*
- *Customer retention*
- *Upsell/cross-sell*
- *Investor/stockholder expectations*
- *ROI*
- *Traffic*
- *Targets/goals*
- *Seasonality*
- *New products*
- *Margins*
- *Cash flow*
- *Growth*
- *Customer loyalty*
- *Competition*
- *Churn*
- *Channel support*
- *More/better customers*
- *Service*
- *Consideration*
- *Infrastructure*
- *Culture*
- *Technology advances*
- *Personnel/management*
- *Exit plan*
- *Market share*
- *Employee morale*
- *Product quality*
- *Security*
- *Reputation*
- *Brand image*
- *Awareness*
- *Retailer support*
- *Price*

In our earlier example of reengineering the RFP for Slip-ons Footwear, some important business issues were clear:

- New competitors have entered Slip-ons' niche
- Historic competitors have increased their marketing investments to defend, while Slip-ons has not
- Inflation has helped erode Slip-ons' price impression
- Slip-ons is missing their financial goals
- Units and revenue are flat
- The client expects a media plan that can drive +5% unit and revenue growth

## Business Issues Are Often Hiding in Plain Sight

Many RFPs are not as clear. In such cases, agencies can often uncover business issues in public documents and online research, such as in the notes (from several years ago) below.

> **For Kroger:**
>
> In head-to-head competition, Kroger has been able to fend off its biggest competitors, which include **Walmart, Albertsons,** and **Aldi.** Kroger is an exceptional competitor, as its latest quarterly results prove. The problem for Kroger is that the game has changed. No longer is Kroger competing head-to-head against traditional grocery retailers; **Kroger must now compete against Amazon — and Amazon isn't playing the same game.**

In the note above, Kroger's emerging business issue was clear: after competing head-to-head with traditional retailers for many years, they now had to contend with a very different type of competitor (Amazon).

**Opportunities to Address:** An agency pitching Kroger at this time could have addressed the challenge of competing with Amazon.

### For Kimberly-Clark:

For the first nine months of 2019, Kimberly-Clark's **sales of $13.9 billion were down slightly. Changes in foreign currency exchange rates reduced sales by 4 percent**, and business exits in conjunction with the 2018 **Global Restructuring Program reduced sales slightly.** Organic sales increased 4 percent. Net selling prices rose 4 percent and product mix improved 1 percent, while **volumes fell 1 percent.**

Kimberly-Clark had mixed results. Prices and organic sales increased, while exchange rates and restructuring had a negative impact on sales. Notably, volume was off.

**Opportunities to Address:** An agency pitching Kimberly-Clark at this time could have addressed the challenge of stimulating volume growth.

### For Jones Soda:

Jones Soda had an important **infusion of capital and resources** through the HeavenlyRx strategic financing, along with continued progress in **building out our sales and marketing teams.** We have also made some exciting steps forward in 2020, becoming the **official craft soda of the Vans Park Series** as we **push to further expand our presence within the skateboarding community.** In addition, we are **rolling out our popular watermelon flavor** to distribution and retail partners across North America following the **positive customer reaction** to the exclusive launch last summer in Canada.

Jones Soda was gaining traction in the skateboarding community and its new watermelon flavor had been well received.

**Opportunities to Address:** An agency pitching Jones Soda at this time could have addressed opportunities like capitalizing on the watermelon flavor success, making even more strides with the skateboarding community, and identifying additional niches like the skateboarding community for further growth.

### For Jersey Mike's:

This past year, Jersey Mike's posted **systemwide same-store sales gains of 6 percent** across its rapidly growing system. The fourth quarter marked **16 consecutive quarters of positive growth**, and the chain **opened 170 units during the fiscal calendar**. It signed deals to **debut another 160 in 2018** – 60 percent from its current system. By 2020, **the 1,300-unit chain expects to have 2,000 restaurants nationwide.**

Jersey Mike's has been on a roll. Strong sales growth and 170 new store openings continued a multi-year growth momentum. Notably, the chain has very significant expansion plans, including opening hundreds of additional stores.

**Opportunities to Address:** An agency pitching Jersey Mike's at this time could have addressed best practices in supporting new store openings.

## Business Issues Lead to Marketing Opportunities

As you begin examining these issues, you need to be able to tie them to marketing goals so that you are sure it's an issue you can actually address. For instance, if you believe that a company can't hire enough people, that's not an issue where most agencies can help. Whatever business issue you define has to be seen in relation to a potential marketing angle of some kind, so that when you start talking about solutions, it's clear how it relates directly to the issue at hand.

Let's say you've identified that a company has a revenue problem. One way to fix that may be to provide more point-of-purchase or in-store materials, as that can help drive revenue. If you know that they have a market share problem, perhaps focusing on their target audience and your advantages versus the competition might be a solution. If they don't have enough traffic to their stores, perhaps geo-targeted advertising might help get more people in the door.

Above all else, the goal is to make sure your agency solutions directly address business needs. Here are some examples:

| BUSINESS ISSUE | POTENTIAL AGENCY SOLUTION |
|---|---|
| Trial | POP/in-store materials |
| Traffic | Promotional radio |
| Customer acquisition | Sampling |
| Purchase frequency | Loyalty card |
| Awareness | Mass media |

Naturally, there are multiple marketing solutions available for every business issue. For example, revenue can be driven through a variety of approaches, such as more compelling advertising, point-of-purchase displays, promotional campaigns, coupons, and cross-sell or upsell programs, to name just a few. The learning gained from the business profile, reengineered RFP, Q&A, and public documents will serve as valuable inspiration, guiding your agency in identifying ways to help the prospect succeed.

---

**EXERCISE: BUSINESS ISSUES**

Consider three specific clients of your agency:

- What are the key business issues facing each firm?
- How have those issues changed over time?
- Do you often engage your clients and prospects in discussions about the prospect's business issues?

# CHAPTER 16
# Pitch Planning: Original Research

If you have the time to invest — meaning as little as two weeks leading up to the pitch — we recommend doing some original research, because it's far more impressive to the prospect. Original research could be any number of things:

- A Facebook poll
- An online survey created on SurveyMonkey
- A target audience panel
- A person-on-the-street interview
- A focus group in your facility

It doesn't have to be a big, elaborate, expensive research study. It's just something where you can gain some useful insight into how the consumer thinks about the company, brand, competition, or category. Prospects are always impressed with original research because it shows a genuine interest in their challenges and a desire to discover specific insight.

It's easy to find the competition for a prospect. It's much more challenging to find existing information about how an audience feels about a brand. This is the place to lean into original research because there are lots of ways to do it that are fast, easy, and cheap. The goal is to get something out, fielded, and back in time to be able to analyze it enough to gain actionable learning.

Another way to leverage this research is to offer it to the prospect for their own use, regardless of whether or not you become their agency of choice. You might put together a synopsis of your findings that are shared during the pitch but could also say, "These are our discoveries, and we'd be happy to share the full scope of our research details if you think it could be helpful."

Extending a genuine offer or favor to a prospect without expecting reciprocation demonstrates authenticity and goodwill. This act of selfless generosity can leave a powerful, enduring impression, potentially fostering trust and strengthening the relationship in the long run.

### PROSPECT-FRIENDLY ACTIONS

**Mark Astone, CEO, Catalyst Marketing Company**

*"9 times out of 10, the client will actually let us do free research for them as part of a pitch, leveraging their database. We'll ask them, 'Hey, we'd like to do a research study. We'll give you the results for free. We don't need any proprietary information. We'll give you the survey, all you have to do is kick it out to your player's club, and then we'll give you the results, and then we can use that in the pitch.' And I think we only had one client ever say no."*

## EXERCISE: BUSINESS ISSUES

Reflecting on the last few big pitches your agency was involved in:

- Did your team take the initiative to do any original research as part of the process? If so, how did you approach gathering that information?
- What key learning emerged from the research you conducted?
- Did you end up incorporating those research findings prominently into your pitch presentation and materials? If so, how did that research help strengthen your proposal?

# CHAPTER 17
# The Written Proposal

A written proposal is often required.

As your agency progresses in discussions with a prospective client, the time has come to deliver a comprehensive written proposal. This may not be the final step in the process — there could be presentations or a Q&A session after the proposal submission, followed by potential negotiations.

Regardless of what comes next, the written proposal is a critical milestone that requires your full attention. This is your opportunity to make a standout impression and demonstrate that you truly understand the client's business and can provide the ideal solution.

When crafting the proposal, speak directly to the client's unique needs and challenges, using their own language and terminology. Show them that they are your top priority, not just another job. Keep the formatting clean and polished, making the document easy to read and visually appealing.

Remember, this proposal could be the deciding factor that advances your candidacy. Approach it with care, creativity, and a laser focus on meeting the client's specific requirements. This is your chance to shine and convince them that your agency is the perfect partner.

Here's how to craft a written proposal that sells.

## THE KEYS TO WRITING WINNING WRITTEN PROPOSALS

The most effective written proposals share a common thread — they keep the focus squarely on the prospect's specific challenges and needs, rather than just highlighting the agency's own capabilities.

As the wise words of Jon Landeau to Jimmy Iovine suggest, "It's not about you." When wooing a prospective client, the approach should mirror that of a first date — you want to make the other person feel truly heard and understood before talking about yourself.

Imagine meeting someone for the first time and immediately launching into a long list of your own skills and accomplishments. The person across from you would likely tune out and start planning their escape. The same dynamic applies to winning new business.

Prospects want to feel respected, understood, and assured that you're the right partner to solve their problems. Only after you've thoroughly demonstrated your comprehension of their challenges should you then showcase how your agency's capabilities align to deliver the ideal solution.

The most compelling proposals keep the client's needs at the forefront, speaking their language and making them feel like your top priority. This client-centric approach is the most effective way to earn their trust and business.

How do you do that in a written proposal? The trick is to organize your proposal in a way that highlights just how focused your agency is on the prospect's business and their challenges. If you do this well, your written proposal will be compelling. It will stand out from the competition as the competitive proposals will undoubtedly focus more on the agency before addressing the prospect's needs.

## Both the Content AND the Order are Critical

We've found that the order and structure of your written proposal or RFI response can significantly impact its effectiveness. That's why we've developed a specialized Mercer Island Group approach to crafting these critical documents.

This unique methodology is designed to differentiate your agency by keeping the focus squarely on the prospect's needs and challenges. Rather than simply listing your own capabilities, we guide you to deliver the content in a more thoughtful, customized way that resonates deeply with the client.

Most agencies take a generic, self-centered approach. Our proven process, on the other hand, ensures your proposal speaks the client's language and demonstrates a genuine understanding of their pain points. This client-centric focus is what helps our clients consistently advance to the next round of the election process.

By following our strategic framework, you'll create a proposal that stands out and compels the prospect to see your agency as the ideal partner to solve their specific problems. It's an approach that gets results — helping you rise above the competition and win the business.

## THE ELEMENTS OF WINNING WRITTEN PROPOSALS

Crafting a truly compelling, prospect-centric written proposal starts with a strategic structure that helps your agency stand out. The key is organizing the content in a way that keeps the focus firmly on the client's needs and challenges.

## Mercer Island Group's Prospect-Friendly Written Proposal Format

*1. Cover Letter*

*2. Business Issues & Implications*

*3. Agency Analysis & Strategy*

*4. Recommended Solutions*

*5. Case Studies*

*6. Relevant Experience*

*7. Agency Background*

*8. Next Steps*

*9. Appendices*

With this framework in mind, let's dive into each section and discuss how to ensure your written proposal is genuinely compelling for the prospective client.

1. **Cover letter:** Every written submission should start with a prospect-friendly cover letter. We read hundreds of written proposals each year. These proposals often lack a cover letter and miss an opportunity to stand out. This can be a huge mistake.

   When responding to a request for a written proposal, your agency is likely competing against multiple submissions from other firms. And the sobering reality is that your prospective client may not have the time or bandwidth to read every word of each proposal in detail.

   This means there's a real risk that some of the key content you've carefully crafted could get overlooked or missed entirely. Your prospect might skim through the documents, focusing only on the salient points.

   As a result, it's critical that you structure your proposal in a way that ensures the most important information is prominently featured and immediately accessible. Key messages and differentiators need to jump off the page, making a strong impression even if the document isn't read thoroughly.

The structure, formatting, and visual design of your proposal should work in harmony to guide the reader's eye and highlight your agency's distinctive value. By making it easy for the client to quickly grasp your core offering and capabilities, you increase the chances of your submission rising to the top.

Remember, you're not just competing on the quality of your work — you're also vying for your prospect's limited attention. A strategically crafted, prospect-focused proposal can make all the difference in advancing to the next round.

A prospect-friendly cover letter can help your agency stand out. It sets you up for success and can help you make a great impression.

In our experience, these are the most impactful points agencies should include in their cover letter:

a) Express enthusiasm and appreciation for the consideration. Something as simple as: "Thank you for inviting AGENCY X to your agency selection process and for the time you will be investing in reviewing our submission."

b) Demonstrate your understanding: Recap the business issues and implications that the prospect has shared.

   Business issues are the key challenges or opportunities a company is facing. They are not "nice to haves." They are clear and present dangers and prominent opportunities. (i.e., revenue, market share, increased competition, store traffic, etc.)

c) Mention, in one sentence, how you have addressed similar issues for specific clients in the past. In other words, a caselet. A simple reference (or name-drop) will do, if you include the following:

The brand you supported
The business challenge
The strategy or tactic the agency used
The outcome

**Example:** "This challenge and our approach would be similar to how we helped COMPANY A shift to a new family-focused target audience and increase ecommerce sales by +573%."

If you hit each of these items, not only will you have written an appreciative letter that demonstrates your capabilities; you will also prove that you understand their business issues and know how to create solutions.

2. **Business Issues & Implications:** Dedicate this section to outlining what you've heard from the client. Identify the issues and/or opportunities that the client is looking to solve. This immediately demonstrates to the client that you've listened to them and really "get" them.

3. **Analysis & Strategic Insights:** Provide your agency's analysis of the situation. Make sure that it adds value and clearly communicates what it means to the client. Do this by laying out your key learnings and opportunities you uncovered after diving into data and research. Include a review of the consumer/customer, competition/industry, and brand. Highlight the key insights you've identified and developed.

4. **Recommended Solutions:** Based on your deep understanding of the business issues the client is facing,

you've developed a comprehensive set of recommended solutions designed to deliver the results the client needs. Outline the key components of your proposed approach and solution.

5. **Case Studies:** Most requests will include an ask for case studies. Carefully select your case studies and customize each one:
   1. State how the case study is relevant to the prospect's business issue and what learning applies to the prospect.
   2. Include an overview of the objectives, goals, work, and results.
   3. Explain why the approach was taken and how it exemplifies your distinctive agency positioning.
6. **Relevant Experience:** At the heart of your proposed solution is a talented, experienced team that is ideally suited to drive the success of the client's business. This is where you introduce the key members who will be dedicated to the account. Include bios of key agency executives and day-to-day team members, highlighting their relevant skills, experience, and how they will contribute to the client's success. In addition to this seasoned team, you can also introduce what we call an interaction process for elaborating effectively with your clients. Outline your agency's client engagement approach (interaction philosophy), including examples, processes, and tools used to ensure a seamless, productive partnership.
7. **Agency Background:** Keep this section short and sweet. Cover the basics about your agency, your agency capabilities (as relevant to the client's issues), and your current/past client experience (as relevant to the client's issues).

8. **Next Steps:** Thank the client for the opportunity to present your proposed solution and demonstrate your capabilities. Be sure to express your true excitement about the prospect of partnering with their organization to drive meaningful, lasting impact.

9. **Appendices:** This is the spot to include all the additional client-specific requests that you need to cover but don't want the client to dwell on (i.e., estimate, SOW, staffing plan, etc.). You should always make sure you include every item your prospect has asked of you. However, you don't need to put these items at the front of your submission.

If you hit each of these items in this order, you will have written a response that demonstrates your capabilities and holds their attention. You will also prove that you understand their business issues and know how to create solutions.

### Additional Considerations

Sometimes it is unclear whether the order of a written proposal is important to the client. In many cases, clients have no preference if all of their requested items are included. When in doubt, it's best to ask the client directly. If they confirm that the order is not important, follow our recommended format.

Regardless of the structure, clearly indicate where in your response each specific request is addressed. Including a table of contents with page numbers is always the best practice.

A strong written response includes many important elements, and formatting is one of them. Thoughtful formatting can help your firm stand out and highlight what matters most to the client. Your submission may serve as your first impression with a prospect, and when crafted effectively, can set the tone for a productive and lasting relationship.

---

**PROSPECT-FRIENDLY ACTIONS**

**Mark Astone, CEO, Catalyst Marketing Company**

*"In the past, we barely read the RFP. We flat out just assumed everybody has the same needs, and we knew what they were... and so we weren't very disciplined in our process. That's probably one of the bigger things — if not THE biggest thing. Just the discipline to develop a process, to work the process, and not to make a lot of assumptions. Inherently, we're problem-solvers to begin with, but I think we assumed we knew what the problem was, and we knew what the solution was, every time. And that pushes you more towards a canned response versus a custom response. And nobody wants that."*

## SOME PRACTICAL ADVICE

Once you've finalized the content of your proposal, be sure to present it in an engaging and visually appealing way.

Consider using a flexible, graphics-friendly platform such as Keynote or PowerPoint to develop your response. These tools make it easier to incorporate images, charts, and other visual elements. In contrast, Word documents often appear less engaging and may not capture the reader's attention as effectively.

Be concise and make good use of white space. Give the reader time to breathe! And keep in mind that the longer your response, the less likely the prospect will read it in its entirety. You do yourself a favor by being concise, as the odds are higher that the prospect will read the full proposal.

Use clear organization techniques to package your response

and improve navigation. Include a table of contents and page numbers to make it easier for the prospect to browse, discuss, and share your proposal.

**EXERCISE: THE WRITTEN PROPOSAL**

- Does your agency have a standard framework for written proposals?
- Given what you learned in this chapter, how might you change your written proposal format?
- Do your written proposals lead with information about the agency, or do they dive right into the prospect's business challenges?

# CHAPTER 18
# How to Run a Prospect-Friendly Tissue Session

The tissue session is frequently a pivotal stage in a competitive agency review.

The term "tissue session" dates back to a time before the digital era. Creatives — typically art directors — would sketch out ideas on tracing paper, also known as tissue paper, to present their concepts. This allowed them to quickly mark up, erase, and revise their work in real time. In essence, the tissue session served as an early form of what we now recognize as a modern collaboration platform.

In a modern agency review, the tissue session now represents any midpoint work session where the agency can present early strategies or tactics and get feedback from the prospective client. They serve as an important check-in during the review, and when done well, represent a significant opportunity for both the agency and client.

How can agencies use a tissue session to enhance their chances of winning?

Tissue sessions generally don't follow a strict agenda: this is the agency's opportunity to demonstrate progress and for the prospect to get a feel for what it's like to collaborate with the agency. We usually let the agency team take the lead and run the meeting as they see fit.

Drawing from our experience with these crucial sessions, it's most effective to focus on:

- Early thinking about the business challenge
- Early strategic approaches
- Preliminary solution concepts

Hopefully, the early work and thinking your team is doing will be the prompts for a hearty conversation.

Having experienced hundreds of tissue sessions, we have identified the following best practices for agencies.

**Tissue Session Best Practices for Agencies**

1. **Begin by revisiting the business challenge or opportunity.** This should serve as the foundation for any marketing initiative. By starting here, the agency underscores its commitment to helping the client address critical business issues. This is also an opportune moment to highlight the agency's value, especially if your work has uncovered key opportunities related to the client's challenge.

2. **Provide a brief overview of the strategic analysis conducted.** Explain how this analysis has generated insights that can drive impactful tactics. What did you discover about the target audience, competition, or the brand? Share the key insights that emerged from your research.

3. **Introduce early tactical ideas, if relevant.** Clearly articulate how these tactics are informed by the insights you've developed and how they will help address the client's business challenge.

4. **Engage the client during the meeting.** Ask thought-provoking questions to move the discussion forward,

such as, "Which aspects of this analysis resonate with you, and which parts might you have questions about?"

5. **Conclude the session with a summary.** Recap the key points discussed, including the client's input, and outline what they can expect in the next meeting. Ensure the client is aligned with your summary before wrapping up.

A well-planned tissue session is a fantastic opportunity for your agency to stand out. Share early thinking about the business challenge, early strategies that can solve the challenge, and even early solution ideas.

And ask for feedback!

Prospects appreciate seeing how an agency incorporates their input. Make sure to actively seek feedback and demonstrate how you've addressed it, giving them a clear sense of their role in shaping the process.

---

**EXERCISE: TISSUE SESSIONS**

- How do you approach a tissue session today?
- How might you adjust your approach to tissue sessions based on what we've discussed in this chapter?

# CHAPTER 19
# The Prospect-Friendly Pitch Presentation

A lot of agencies hate to pitch, which is understandable. It can be awkward, uncomfortable, expensive, and exhausting. And for many smaller agencies, it's outside the norm of how they usually land business, with many partnerships coming together through referrals and simple meetings to clarify wants and needs. But if winning more business is the goal, being able to deliver a compelling presentation can be a key to company growth.

## The invitation means you belong at the party.

If you're a smaller agency (or any agency, really) that has landed an opportunity to pitch to a prospect that might seem out of your league (bigger brand name, bigger budget, etc.), you first need to take a deep breath and accept that you deserve to be in the room just as much as anyone. Something got you in the door, which means the potential client is just as eager to hear your thoughts as anyone else's. Pitching is hard and can be incredibly intimidating but always remember to shift your focus away from yourself and onto the client's need. If you see the pitch as an opportunity to help someone instead of to sell your skills, it creates an air of compassion and empathy that the prospect can feel.

It's also good to keep in mind that bigger isn't always better. We've been a part of hundreds of pitches and have often witnessed small agencies pitching against some of the most recognizable names in the world and winning big business with companies like LG Electronics, Kumon, and Zillow. The size of your agency matters less than the preparation, presentation, strategic solutions, and prospect friendliness of your pitch.

**Focus on the prospect.**

So, why is pitching such a challenge for so many agencies? As we've discussed throughout this book, a lot of it comes down to a fundamental misunderstanding of who and what the pitch is really for. When approached as a sales pitch — where the agency focuses on showcasing their skills and achievements in hopes of dazzling the client — it can come across as a superficial dog-and-pony show. "Look at us! We're incredible! Let us wow you with our brilliance!" This approach often backfires, closing more doors than it opens, because it overlooks the most crucial aspect: being genuinely prospect-friendly.

As you start to build your next pitch, remember to take your agency out of it as much as possible. There is room for a little self-promotion but it's a lot less than most agencies present. Put yourself in the client's shoes as much as possible and consider what they need to see and hear. Your reputation got you in the room, so don't ruin it by stealing the spotlight away from the client and their business needs.

Be confident but also gracious, empathetic, and sincere. Don't tell them you're good. Show them.

## THE PROSPECT-FRIENDLY PITCH

It can seem daunting to build a pitch from a blank canvas, especially if you're not familiar with how much or how little to include. We've seen 200-page decks and 10-slide presentations. As you might imagine, both have failed for different but similar reasons: failure to put the client first.

There's a better approach: **The Prospect-Friendly Pitch.**

## Mercer Island Group's Prospect-Friendly Pitch Format

A prospect-friendly pitch has nine basic steps:

1. *Agency Introductions*
2. *Client Introductions*
3. *Manage Expectations*
4. *Mutual Agenda*
5. *Address Business Issues*
6. *The Five Slides*
7. *Solutions*
8. *Closing*
9. *Next Steps*

As you start to build from this outline, repeatedly ask yourself, "Is this about the agency or the client?" Odds are good you're going to find it challenging to slash how much you want to talk about yourself, but if you stay focused on the prospect and deliver a clear and concise client-centric pitch, you will greatly improve your odds of landing more business.

1. **Agency Introductions:** The pitch typically begins with the agency owner or a senior executive from the leadership team. When introducing the team, use a slide that features a photo of each agency member present, along with their titles. It's also a good idea to briefly explain how each person will play a direct role in supporting the prospect's business.

   Another option that we highly recommend is the use of placemats instead of, or in addition to, this slide.

The placemat is a simple printout that can include:

- Pictures of each member of the presenting team
- Their roles in the business
- Agency positioning
- Key clients
- Size, awards, locations

Keep headshots clean and professional. We've seen agencies use photos of dogs, babies, cartoons, or even types of cheese for introductions. While that might be entertaining for an internal team-building activity, it has no place in a pitch. Simply state who you are and the role you'll play in the client's business.

Be careful about any additional "flair" you might bring to your introductions. Years ago, we managed a review for CenturyLink, a privately held, Fortune 100 company headquartered in Louisiana. They are fiercely proud of being from the South. When a New York-based agency came in to pitch, each person on the agency's team shared a story about their experience in or perception of the South. It was inauthentic and pandering. The pitch was over before it even began because it was so poorly received by the prospect. It seemed disingenuous.

While it may seem obvious, it's crucial to ensure your pitch team reflects the diversity of the prospect's company and the market demographic they serve. Today, clients expect agencies to have teams that mirror the diversity of their target audiences and the broader population they're targeting. This isn't just important when pitching to companies that represent women or minorities — it's now a universal expectation, regardless of who's sitting across the table. If your team lacks diversity, address it.

Also, make sure that everyone attending from the agency pitch team is given an opportunity to speak, especially during the sections of the presentation that will handled by their skill set. We've seen pitches where the single woman on the team has been relegated to advancing the slides on the presentation, even though she's been introduced as the key day-to-day contact.

2. **Client Introductions:** The agency team has introduced themselves, and now it's time for one of the most critical moments in the presentation: the client introductions.

   This might sound surprising but stay with us for a moment.

   After the agency introductions are completed, ask the client team to introduce themselves by saying something like this:

   *"As we dive into our presentation, we'd like to make sure it is as on the money as possible. Please introduce yourself, tell us what your role is on the business, and one thing you'd like to accomplish during our time together."*

   As the client team introduces themselves, make sure to capture the "one thing" comments. Take good notes, and if possible, capture them for all to see on a whiteboard or flipchart.

   With that one question, you will achieve something that no other presenting agency likely will:

   - You've gotten the client talking within the first five minutes of your pitch.
   - You've captured valuable information about what's top of mind for the client.
   - By capturing the responses, you've demonstrated how your agency actively listens to their needs.

This is an incredibly powerful technique! Beyond the benefits we've just outlined, it's also highly possible that some attendees haven't been deeply involved in the pitch process and may want to address topics that were not fully covered in the RFP. One of these individuals could even be the most senior decision-maker, who may have entirely different priorities. By asking the "one thing" question, you'll be the only agency with the opportunity to tackle important issues that weren't captured in the RFP.

**PROSPECT-FRIENDLY ACTIONS**

**Mark Astone, CEO, Catalyst Marketing Company**

*"I went around the room and did introductions, and I asked them to tell me what they wanted to get out of the meeting. And they looked at me a little funny. But doggone on it they did it. And not only did they do it, they spilled their guts. And we ended up jumping on multiple things that they had said later on in the pitch. The vice chair said, 'This is impressive, nobody's ever asked us that and listened to what we had to say.' I'm convinced that's part of the reason why we won."*

3. **Manage Expectations and Shared Agenda:** With the introductions out of the way, the next step is to confirm alignment with the client on what you plan to cover.

   You'll have already compiled a list of key business issues during your preparation, based on their brief, the Q&A, your own analysis, and their responses to the "one thing" question. Display that list (on a slide, flipchart, or whiteboard) and say:

   *"Based on our preparation and your thorough briefing, we've identified these critical business issues for your company. We plan to address these in today's discussion. Is there anything else we should add to this list?"*

As an example, you might say to a retail client, "From our discussions to date, we have heard that you need to build traffic, add store baskets, and fend off a new competitor. Is there anything else we should add to that list?"

At this stage, they may agree with your list or even suggest additions. Once the list is finalized, say:

*"Our plan for the remainder of our time today is to focus on these business issues. Let's dive in."*

Now, you've established alignment on what matters most and what you'll cover during the discussion. In other words, you've created a shared agenda.

4. **Present Business Issues and Analysis:** Now, you transition into the core of the presentation. This is where you guide the prospect through the analysis you've conducted and explain what it means for their business.

   Begin by demonstrating a clear understanding of the prospect's specific needs. Present your strategy, data, and analysis, backed by detailed insights into their company, target audience, competition, and brand. Share any proprietary research you've conducted and how these findings have shaped your solutions.

   Your thorough analysis should ideally lead to a powerful strategic insight that drives your recommendations. This insight, along with its implications for your solutions, can help your agency distinguish itself from the competition.

   At this point, you're ready to introduce your proposed tactics (creative, a media plan, PR plan, etc.) and the prospect is leaning forward. They are on the edge of their seats, eager to see how you will solve their business issue.

   This is an ideal moment for a brief pause.

5. **The Five Slides:** When you attend a live theater performance, the usher hands you a playbill as you enter. You settle into your seat, perhaps flipping through it briefly, but you're mostly eager for the show to begin. The playbill doesn't hold much interest at this point.

   Then the performance starts, and you're captivated! By intermission, you recall the playbill and now feel a fresh curiosity to dive into it. Who's playing the lead role? What's their background? Have they performed on Broadway? Suddenly, you're interested in the actors because you've seen them in action — they've come to life in context.

   Similarly, talking about your agency too early in a presentation can be a snooze-fest — it's like listening to Charlie Brown's teacher. But after demonstrating your deep focus on the client's business, presenting insightful analysis, and sharing a compelling strategic insight, they'll be far more open to learning about your agency.

   To smoothly transition from your strategic work to your proposed tactics, you might say something like:

   *"We understand you have other options, and we're truly honored that you're considering our agency. To put our recommended solutions into context, we'd like to spend just a few minutes to tell you about the agency before we introduce those solutions."*

And then you present the Five Slides. These are the Five Slides we discussed in detail in Chapter 8. Again, there are always five, and ONLY five:

1. Agency Philosophy
2. Agency Strategic Process
3. Agency Interaction Process
4. Agency Capabilities
5. Agency Client Logos

6. **Solutions:** After this short reminder of what your agency brings to the table, give a recap of the overall insight and then reveal your brilliant solutions that ladder back to the strategy.

   This is often the riskiest part of any pitch because it's typically developed without client feedback or revisions. It's a significant leap of faith that can either elevate or derail your presentation. This is why **manifesto videos** can be so impactful — they help convey your vision in a compelling, client-focused way.

   When presenting your creative solution, frame it as a **story** that mirrors your agency's process. Stories are far more engaging and memorable than raw data or statistics. Walk the client through how the solution works and consistently tie it back to their specific business challenges. Most importantly, ensure the client is following along and understands how everything connects to their needs.

   It's common for agencies to want to include a **full case study** to demonstrate how they've successfully tackled similar challenges in the past. Unless explicitly requested, we advise against this. Why? Because your past case studies are about your experience not the prospect's current situation. Focus on their needs, not your history.

   Instead of dedicating several important minutes to talking about someone else, keep it focused on the prospect by referencing past successes quickly and succinctly in a way that directly ties to the current conversation. As an example, *"Here we're recommending that you use a heavy digital programmatic buy, like we successfully did for PetCo."* This gives credibility to your solution by proving you have solved a similar problem with positive results. This becomes essentially a "caselet" of a case study as you share only the challenge you faced, the solution you created, and the results. This doesn't necessarily have to be a separate slide. It can just be part of the dialogue, or a box on the slide where it is specifically relevant.

It's also important to include an overview of how you will measure success for the concepts presented. It's one thing to share a great marketing strategy, but the prospect needs to fully understand how the investment will be quantified.

*"Before we wrap up, let us share with you exactly how we plan to gauge our strategy's achievements."*

7. **Closing & Next Steps:** Finish the pitch with a clear summary of the points and solutions presented. Oftentimes, this is when the agency owner or most senior leader on the pitch team would again take the lead. Go over the shared agenda from the beginning of the meeting to ensure everything was addressed. This is your opportunity to reiterate the benefits and synopsize how well your solution matches each of the items listed on the shared agenda created together at the top of the pitch.

   Thank them for their time and consideration, and make sure to clearly express your enthusiasm for the opportunity to work with them.

   *"This is a significant decision, and it deserves a thoughtful and thorough process. As you weigh your options, we want you to know just how honored we would be to partner with you. As a next step, we'd love to host you in our offices so you can experience firsthand what it is like to collaborate with us."*

---

## A FEW BONUS SUGGESTIONS

### Leadership's Role

At some point, the agency owner will likely turn the pitch over to other members of their team. At that time, it is the leader's responsibility to remain quiet yet supportive for the rest of the pitch. No jumping in to clarify or adjust information. This creates the perception that the agency leader isn't confident in their own people. And if they're not confident in it, why should the prospect be?

Additionally, the owner should remain engaged and not glance at their phone or step out to take a call. Just because they're not running the presentation doesn't mean the prospect isn't taking note of their engagement.

### Take Notes

Clients and prospects feel better if you're taking notes, so when they're talking, write it down. You're acknowledging their input, feedback, and viewpoints, and showing interest in their questions and concerns. Make eye contact as they speak, glancing down to jot down keywords. Remember, you're taking notes, not dictation.

### You Did It

Pitching doesn't have to feel like a "necessary evil." In fact, it can even be — dare we say it — enjoyable. The less you focus on what your agency wants and the more you center the conversation around the prospect's needs, the more rewarding the experience becomes for everyone involved. It shifts from being about selling something to genuinely solving a problem. Saying "**Let us help**" creates a far more inviting dialogue than simply asking "**Give us work**."

## EXERCISE: PITCH PRESENTATION

Gather your team and explore the following questions:

- How does your typical pitch framework compare to the one outlined in this chapter? What are the most significant differences?
- What's the biggest challenge your agency faces when creating the ideal pitch deck?
- What concerns do you have about the approach recommended in this chapter? Is there anything about this method that gives you pause or feels worrisome?

# CHAPTER 20
# Staffing the Prospect-Friendly Pitch

Our friend Scott Davis, an EVP at the excellent independent media agency Harmelin, once challenged us to write about agency pitch staffing. Here is a lightly edited version of his note:

> *"If I may be so bold as to suggest a topic that's of particular interest (and frustration) to me — it's about how early in the process prospects are now asking to 'meet the team that will work on the business.' I completely understand the need for a company to not just meet the agency, but also the individuals they'd be collaborating with. However, this request is coming earlier and earlier in the process — a team org chart is often asked for at the RFI stage, and the team is typically expected at the first capabilities meeting.*
>
> *Given that a pitch can span four to six months, this is incredibly challenging for us as an agency, because none of us has a pool of people sitting idle, waiting for their next assignment. It feels unfair (in my opinion) to ask us to put a team 'on ice' for months when there's only a one-in-four chance of winning the business. I'm curious if you're seeing this trend as well, and since you have the benefit of both client and agency perspectives, I'd love to hear your thoughts."*

Here is our response…

We think there is a happy medium that works for both clients and agencies.

Before we get to that, let's take a moment to highlight how we have gotten to this point where clients are hoping to see the people that will work on the business all through a very long pitch. It seems the largest agencies have trained senior marketers to beware of this practice. Several years ago, we saw "the largest media agency in the country" send the same pitch team to three different clients in six months. The presenters were accomplished, smart, articulate, and great on their feet. They were all impressive presenters. Unfortunately, they were all SVP department heads in this agency of several thousand employees. The pitches were amazing, yet they lost two out of three. In the two losses, the prospect team walked away thinking, "We'll never see these people again." There is simply no big-agency business model where such senior execs regularly work on a small or mid-sized client.

Prospects despise the bait-and-switch tactic, where an agency sends a pitch team packed with senior, experienced, and talented presenters who, after winning the business, are never seen again.

So, what's the right team for a pitch? What's the happy medium that works for both agencies and clients? There's an important distinction between *working on the business* and being the *primary day-to-day staffer* for a specific function. It's unlikely clients expect the primary day-to-day person from each function to be involved throughout the entire pitch process. Instead, they want to meet the people who will be responsible for the work and are close enough to the day-to-day operations to speak confidently about the account.

This is a nuanced difference, but one that we believe helps agencies navigate the challenges of pitch staffing while still allowing clients to get a sense of the team they'll be working with. It's about striking the right balance—showing the right level of expertise and involvement without overcommitting resources prematurely.

Here is an easy test an agency can use in judging if the team is a pitch team or not: if (other than the management sponsor) most executives on the pitch team are not included in the SOW, it's a pitch team.

In our experience, most clients do not need to see, during the entire pitch, the heaviest billing executive from each discipline. Rather, an ideal pitch team has:

- The day-to-day agency team member that the client will work with
- Execs from each key discipline that are senior enough to be accountable for their function's support and will bill the account
- A diverse makeup of individuals representative of the prospect's target audience
- A senior executive or owner who vouches for the agency's commitment

The agency world, much like other professional services, is characterized by subtle differentiations and limited brand recognition. Agencies frequently pitch for new business, and the ability to secure more than their "fair share" of opportunities is crucial for profitability. Running a compelling pitch — particularly in a competitive environment — is essential to achieving a high win rate. Properly staffing a pitch can often be the deciding factor between success and failure.

## EXERCISE: PITCH PRESENTATION

Gather your team and explore the following questions:

- How do you currently staff your pitches?
- What adjustments are you considering to improve how you staff your pitches?
- Does agency leadership play a role beyond just opening and closing pitches? Is there a way, given your team's structure, to reduce their reliance on leadership for anything other than these bookend tasks?

# CHAPTER 21
# The Virtual Pitch

The year 2020 delivered a series of disruptive lessons that forced everyone to pivot quickly and decisively. COVID-19 permanently altered how we view our lives, both personally and professionally. The interruption of "business as usual" pushed even the most resistant organizations to explore virtual solutions to survive.

For some agencies, this shift was particularly challenging. Many had long believed that being in the room — the in-person dynamic — was essential to winning new business. Agencies that once doubted their ability to operate online were compelled to adapt. In the process, they discovered how much time, energy, and money could be saved by moving certain interactions, including pitches, to a virtual format.

To seize these opportunities, agencies must evolve. How do you effectively pitch your agency without face-to-face meetings? A virtual pitch demands unique strategies to help your agency stand out and secure the win.

While nearly all the insights we've shared in this book still apply to online presentations, there are a few additional elements — specific to virtual settings — that you'll want to incorporate to ensure your success.

## Master the Technology

There are numerous professional web conferencing platforms available for your presentations, and as an agency you'll need to be proficient in all the major ones. Why? Because the prospect may dictate the platform they prefer. Relying solely on your favorite platform and mastering it isn't enough — each platform has its own strengths, weaknesses, and user experience (UX). You need to be comfortable navigating any of the major platforms to ensure you can confidently deliver your presentation, no matter what tool.

At the same time, ensure your team is prepared with a backup plan, should it become necessary due to technical or other issues outside your control. It's a good idea to have the pitch deck ready to be distributed digitally in case that becomes necessary.

### Adjust Your Materials

This is a crucial opportunity to refine the look and feel of your presentation to ensure it authentically represents the client. Use imagery that's highly specific to their company, target audience, and brand identity.

Online presentations differ significantly from in-person presentations. For instance, participants' screen sizes can vary widely, from a 13-inch laptop to a 7-inch tablet or even a smartphone. It's essential to ensure your presentation is clear and legible across all these devices.

Unlike a conference room screen, smaller screens demand a different approach to slide design for effective communication. Your slides must be optimized for these smaller displays. Avoid cluttered or overly detailed slides — no eye charts! Keep them clean, concise, and visually impactful.

### Dress Professionally

A digital presentation may feel like a more casual environment, but you shouldn't treat it as such. Dress just as you would if the presentation were in person. Not only does being fully professionally dressed help you feel fully professionally present, but it eliminates any awkward moments that could arise if circumstances were to change so that your full attire was revealed accidentally.

### Rehearse Differently

Begin by pre-planning the essential components of your presentation, including:

- **Each presenter's content:** Smooth transitions between speakers are crucial — plan them in advance.
- **Q&A management:** Decide how and when to handle questions (e.g., during or after the presentation).
- **Opening and closing:** Craft a strong introduction to grab attention and a compelling conclusion to leave a lasting impression.

By mapping out these key elements, you'll ensure a polished and seamless presentation.

Each agency team member should participate from their own computer in their own private room. Prospects have trouble remembering the identity of each presenter when the agency has multiple presenters using a single screen.

Conduct a formal dress rehearsal using the exact technology platform that will be used in the actual presentation. Invite other agency team members to play the role of the prospect and attend the rehearsal. Ensure your delivery is upbeat and energetic but avoid coming across as overly loud or aggressive.

The team should participate just as your prospect will — remotely, via the online presentation platform. Ideally, have different team members view the presentation on various devices such as a desktop monitor, laptop, tablet, and smartphone to ensure the message is consistently clear and effective, regardless of the device used.

Run through the entire presentation without any interruptions or feedback first. Deliver it exactly as you plan to in the actual pitch — don't just talk through what you intend to say but perform the full pitch as if it's the real thing. This will help you get comfortable with the language, transitions, and flow, while also revealing areas that need improvement. Time each section and the overall presentation to ensure it fits within the allotted timeframe.

Refine your pitch based on your team's feedback and rehearse again to polish your delivery and address any remaining issues.

**Build In Opportunities for Interaction**

Interaction does not happen as spontaneously in a virtual environment. Most of these presentation platforms only allow one speaker at a time, so you may not always be aware when someone has a question or comment. To alleviate this, the agency must ask for reactions and input along the way and suggest that prospects also "raise their hands" or use the chat function to post questions. Plan engaging questions to ask at the end of each section. Some sample questions that work well include:

- "How does this align with your thinking?"
- "Given that we have prepared with limited data and access to your information, what else should we have considered based on your experience?"
- "How does our insight about your customer feel based on your knowledge of the business?"

The key to these questions is to avoid yes/no responses. Instead, frame your prompts in an active and engaging way. Use phrases like "how" and "what else" to encourage more and detailed answers. This approach fosters deeper conversation and provides richer insights.

### Think Digitally

Even if you do land that coveted in-person pitch, it's a good idea to create your pitch with these digital requirements in mind. Things can change at the last minute, and you could be asked to present online rather than in person. You don't want to find yourself suddenly "winging it" without knowing for sure that the presentation is coming across as you intended or to realize at the last minute that it becomes jumbled when viewed on a cellphone.

Being digital-ready also makes it easy to share the presentation with a prospect, should they ask ... and, of course, if they ask, that's always a good sign.

### Toss the Script

It is incredibly obvious when a virtual presenter is using a script. Don't. It diminishes your presence and impression.

---

### EXERCISE: PITCH REHEARSAL

- Does your agency rehearse virtual pitches?
- Do members of your team pitch from a script?
- Is your agency ready to pitch regardless of the teleconference platform?

# CHAPTER 22
# Tips, Tricks, and Magnificent Extras

Tips, tricks, and extra touches to elevate your pitch from good to great.

## The Manifesto Video

When crafting your in-person or virtual pitch, consider incorporating a manifesto video. While not mandatory, these videos can be a powerful tool to brilliantly sell your insight when used appropriately. They add a dynamic, memorable element to your presentation, helping your ideas resonate more deeply with the audience.

If you're going to include a manifesto video, it should come after the Five Slides.

After the Five Slides, you recap the big strategic insight that you uncovered just before the Five Slides and then introduce the manifesto video before presenting solutions.

This "video mood board" helps set the tone for how you want the prospect to think and feel when you present the creative work. When done well, it can act as a safety net for your creative proposal. We've seen it happen more than once: a compelling manifesto video so effectively captures the essence of the brand that it can sell the agency, even if the creative that follows doesn't fully hit the mark. By demonstrating that you understand how the company wants their audience to feel, you make a stronger impression than simply focusing on how they want an ad to look.

McCann created one of the best examples of this approach for Ulta Beauty in 2018. The video that was released to the public is incredibly close to what McCann presented to the client, and it shows how amazing the pitch was that they were able to turn all this strategic work into a video that encapsulates everything they wanted the audience to feel about their campaign.

And the response? After McCann played the video, the client paused and then asked to watch it again. McCann even used Alessia Cara's empowerment anthem "Scars to Your Beautiful" in their pitch. The Ulta Beauty team loved the manifesto so much that they bought the rights to the song and produced a fully original version of the manifesto idea for TV and digital video.

McCann's insight, "You don't come to Ulta Beauty because you want to be beautiful, you come because you already are," elevated the Ulta Beauty strategy. The manifesto worked in the pitch because the Ulta Beauty team felt understood. They really appreciated that with McCann, "the possibilities are beautiful" (a line from the manifesto).

How do you create a manifesto video?

Creating a manifesto video isn't just for large, big-city agencies. Small agencies can also pull this off if it aligns with the prospect's needs. Thanks to technological advancements, there are now low-budget, high-gloss options that can essentially turn your team into a mini production studio.

When it comes to music, you're free to use any track that fits the tone and mood of your video. Since this is for a presentation and not public distribution, you don't need to worry about securing music rights.

This approach is accessible, impactful, and can elevate your pitch to the next level.

It starts with a mood. Agencies have used mood boards for years. Well, this is a mood video. Once you present your strategy, and BEFORE you show your creative, you can present the video as a representation of your insight into the client's brand. "This is how we want our target consumer to feel via the creative we are about to present." It gets your target audience, which is the prospect, feeling what you want them to feel about the work you're about to show them.

**PROSPECT-FRIENDLY ACTIONS**

**Mark Astone, CEO, Catalyst Marketing Company**

*"It's a multiple level thing. One, a picture's worth a thousand words, right? You're clearly demonstrating your creativity. Two, you're demonstrating that you're going the extra mile. Most people don't go in with that, so it's pretty clear that you're working harder for them than someone else. And then, if you hit it, they're like, 'Wow, they get us, they get it, out of the gate, they just get it.' When the client thinks, 'They totally get us,' then it's over at that point. If you get to that point, you've won."*

## Stand Up When You Pitch

A curious behavior has become relatively commonplace in many of the agency pitches we observe: agency execs often sit as they present during pitches.

It is undoubtedly well-intended! These folks probably are hoping for a conversation between their agency and the prospective client, and sitting across a table seems like the natural way to have a deep discussion. Heck, when we go to dinner with friends or have a large corporate meeting we are often sitting across from our friends, family, or work associates.

It's a nice idea in a pitch. And it doesn't work.

Sitting while presenting can detract from the impact of your pitch for several reasons:

1. **Energy Drain:** Sitting tends to sap energy from the room rather than amplify it. It's harder for the presenter to convey enthusiasm and passion while seated.
2. **Limited Connection:** Sitting restricts the presenter's ability to connect with the audience. They're more confined in their gestures and can't take meaningful steps forward to engage in discussions or address questions.
3. **Visual Disconnect:** It can be harder for the prospective client to follow the presentation, especially when slides or a screen are involved. A seated presenter may not be positioned near the screen, making it difficult to gesture effectively toward key content.
4. **Loss of Authority:** Sitting levels the playing field, giving up a position of authority. Standing naturally commands attention and conveys confidence.

Of course, there are exceptions — in very small or intimate meetings, standing might feel out of place.

So, take a stand — literally for your agency! By standing, you'll showcase your conviction in the topic and your agency's recommendations. You'll connect more effectively with your audience and come across as more energetic, enthusiastic, and authoritative.

Stand tall and let your passion shine!

### Don't Lead with Your Tools

Each year, we have the privilege of reviewing numerous agency presentations, witnessing the expertise of talented individuals as they present to our clients. There are, however, occasional missteps that can hinder the potential connection between the agency and the prospective client.

One common issue we've observed is when agencies spend too much time discussing their tools during the pitch. This approach often proves counterproductive, as it shifts the focus away from the client's need and onto the agency's capabilities, rather than building a meaningful bond.

Allow us to elaborate.

Consider this scenario: When you dine at a restaurant for the first time, do you inquire about the chef's choice of knives? When hiring a landscaper, do you question their leaf blower preferences? Likely not. Similarly, when undergoing surgery, you don't concern yourself with the surgeon's preferred scalpel.

Why?

Because individuals seeking services are primarily focused on their business opportunities and challenges. To choose a partner, they want assurance that you truly understand their needs.

Oh, and let's be honest — every agency has tools. Among agencies of similar sizes, these tools are often comparable in terms of capabilities. What truly sets an agency apart isn't the tools themselves, but the people behind them.

Don't get us wrong: tools are important. But while they play a crucial role, they shouldn't take center stage in conversations with prospects. The spotlight should be on your team and their deep understanding of the client's business, challenges, and opportunities. You can certainly mention how tools enhance your strategic thinking but save the detailed tool discussions for when the prospect explicitly shows interest.

Focus on what really matters — your team's expertise and how they'll deliver results for the client.

1. **Align on the Business Challenge or Opportunity:** Start by ensuring you and the client are on the same page about the core issue or opportunity at hand.
2. **Share Insights:** Briefly discuss the insights you've gained from analyzing the target audience, competition, and brand — mentioning specific tools used in the process without going into excessive detail.
3. **Recommend a Strategy:** Present a clear, actionable strategy to address the client's challenge or capitalize on the opportunity.
4. **Illustrate Tactics:** Show how the strategy translates into tangible, actionable tactics that will drive results.

By following this approach, you keep focusing on solving the client's problem while subtly highlighting the tools that support your expertise.

In a nutshell, let your thinking and understanding of the prospect's situation shine, with tools playing a supporting role. If the prospect asks about your tools, provide a concise explanation. If they desire an in-depth discussion, suggest a follow-up session specifically focused on tools.

While tools are essential and play a crucial role in modern marketing, they should not dominate the conversation. Instead, let the spotlight shine on your team's strategic thinking, deep insights, and recommendations. By aligning with the client's goals, sharing valuable insights, and presenting a well-defined strategy, you showcase the true value your agency brings to the table. As discussions naturally progress, you can then seamlessly integrate brief references to the supporting tools that amplify your team's expertise.

Just keep in mind, clients want a partner who really gets what they need and can come up with solid solutions. Let your team and their understanding of the client's world be the main attraction.

---

**EXERCISE: TIPS & TRICKS**

- Has your agency ever created a manifesto video to introduce your strategic insight?
- What was the prospect's reaction?
- What, if anything, would stop you from creating a manifesto video for a critical pitch?

# CHAPTER 23
# Rehearsal

A pitch is a performance. It might not have all the lights, costumes, and orchestra that you'd find at a Broadway musical, but there will certainly be an element of song and dance. You're standing in front of an audience and asking them to think and feel. This takes skill, and skill takes practice. And every pitch is a different kind of show, so it requires rehearsal to be as powerful as it can be.

Unlike in the theater, we don't recommend using a script for your pitch. Relying on a script can make you sound rehearsed and impersonal, which may diminish the impression that you can speak freely and confidently about the subject matter. Simply reciting words from a page doesn't demonstrate a deep or remarkable understanding of the topic.

Instead, rehearsals can help you find the most natural and effective way to communicate your ideas. They allow you to refine your delivery without sounding overly scripted.

Additionally, you may pick up valuable information during the pitch — such as during introductions or early discussions — that require you to adjust your talking points on the spot. If you're tied to a script, making these last-minute changes can be challenging. Staying flexible and responsive shows your ability to think on your feet and adapt to the client's needs in real time.

Focus on knowing your material inside and out, so you can present with confidence and authenticity, rather than relying on a rigid script.

In theater, there are two kinds of rehearsal: a tech rehearsal and a dress rehearsal. Both are equally relevant to your pitch process.

### The Tech Rehearsal

The tech rehearsal is all about ensuring that every technical element functions seamlessly. This includes checking that transitions, videos, music cues, and even handouts run smoothly and without a hitch. The goal is to eliminate any potential glitches that could disrupt the flow of your pitch.

### The Dress Rehearsal

The dress rehearsal is where you run through the entire pitch as if it's the real deal. This means everyone involved — including the agency leader, CEO, or owner — must participate and be fully engaged. Additionally, other team members who aren't part of this specific pitch can sit in and play the role of the prospect. Their job is to take detailed notes on the full experience, providing valuable feedback to refine your presentation.

A proper dress rehearsal isn't about sitting around a table and going through the pitch deck and saying, "And then I'll get up and introduce everyone." Nope. Rather, the pitch team needs to present exactly as you would during the actual presentation, from start to finish, without interruptions or discussions about improvements. Get up and actually introduce everyone. Deliver your part the way you would with the prospect. Plan and deliver your handoffs. Plan and deliver the wrap-up.

This rehearsal approach is crucial for several reasons:

- **It helps you get comfortable with your own material.** Written content often feels different when spoken aloud, and rehearsing ensures you can deliver it naturally and confidently.

- **It familiarizes the team with each other's content.** Everyone gains a full understanding of the material being presented, which helps eliminate unnecessary repetition or omissions.
- **It allows for refinement of the overall flow.** The team can identify and adjust any issues with the sequence or context of the content.
- **It uncovers overlooked errors.** Typos, slide order issues, grainy images, or other mistakes can be spotted and corrected before the actual pitch.

Go through the entire pitch from beginning to end and time it. Once it's over, everyone shares notes with the group, and then you run it again from the top. Wash, rinse, repeat. Do this until you've locked in a comfortable, confident, clear pitch.

### A Word to Agency Owners About Rehearsals

Agency owners or CEOs should fully participate in these dress rehearsals as well as the rest of the pitch team. It's not enough to be the face of the agency; you also have to be an active member of the team. These rehearsals aren't beneath you; they are necessary for your agency's growth and success.

Participating in your agency's rehearsal ensures you have full knowledge and confidence in what's being pitched and how it's being presented.

Often, the agency owner will open and close the pitch, but their actions in between can significantly impact the potential relationship with the prospect. We've seen agency owners interrupt their own team's pitch to clarify, challenge, or even change the information being shared. This sends a troubling message to the prospect: it suggests that the agency owner either doesn't know what their team is presenting or doesn't trust them. Both are damaging impressions to convey during a pitch.

By staying aligned and supportive throughout the presentation, the agency owner can reinforce trust and cohesion, rather than undermining it.

---

**EXERCISE: REHEARSAL**

- Does your team routinely do a tech rehearsal prior to a major pitch?
- Does your team routinely have a full dress rehearsal/ run through exactly as you plan to deliver the pitch?
- What, if anything, has stopped your team from conducting full dress rehearsals?

# CHAPTER 24
# Belief and Conviction Matter in Good Pitches

Marketers and agency execs can learn so much from the world around them. One example is storytelling and persuasiveness: there is so much that agencies can learn from great writers about how to spin a compelling narrative.

Great stories matter. They connect you with your key audiences. They give people a reason to pay attention. And there is more. Great stories presented in a passionate manner can elevate the narrative and increase the odds of your message, recommendation, or pitch connecting.

Our favorite baseball blogger recently wrote about just that. And what she wrote is as relevant to agencies pitching work to prospects or clients as it is to a baseball team engaging its fanbase.

Let's start by introducing baseball's best blogger: Kate Preusser, editor in chief of Lookout Landing, a blog site devoted to the Seattle Mariners. Kate once wrote the following:

> *In an essay about inflection and tone in writing, "You're Really Something," Charles Baxter tells about a family trip to a tourist trap called Dinosaur World, where the affectless teen narrating the tram ride through "a trip back through time" adds a layer of unintended hilarity as the family rumbles along past tableaus of dilapidated dinosaurs, jaws agape, standing in fountains that shoot toilet-cleaner-blue-dyed water. The teenaged guide is baffled when the family*

> *bursts out laughing midway through the tour, ramshackle as it is, but laden with jump scares: "What, you're not scared?" No, the family assures the teen, but not because the plaster on the T-Rex is crumbling and the jungle plants are plastic, but because the entire tour has been delivered in a flat monotone; the suspension of belief is nonexistent, because there was no belief to be suspended in the first place: "None of us at Dinosaur World expected to believe what we were seeing. We expected to be invited to a little party where the host acted as if he believed, or at least was interested in what he was seeing, and was inviting us into that as if."*
>
> *As if. To tell a story, you ask the audience to come into a world you've created; the payment for entry is belief. But to extract that ticket price from an audience, the writer, showman, magician, or baseball team has to believe in what they are doing, to an extent, and be able to perform that belief to others.*

Kate was writing about baseball, but she could have been talking about agency execs. Every day we face audiences with a great deal on their minds, and we ask them to lean in and grace us with their attention. There is a price to gaining that attention and an even greater price to gaining their approval: they need to believe. And for them to believe in your proposal or pitch or point of view, it must be obvious that you believe.

# CHAPTER 25
# The Prospect-Friendly Way to Talk About The Money

Very few clients or agency professionals enjoy discussing money. At best, it's a necessary evil, and at worst, it is nerve-racking and uncomfortable.

And maybe because of the inherent stress involved in these discussions, the norm is to do this poorly. Clients often expect far more than they can afford. Agencies often simply submit a list of tactics along with a cost estimate or a spreadsheet full of staff time and hours associated with a scope. No narrative. No romance. No story about why the investment proposed is important enough that the prospect should buy.

In these situations, neither the agencies nor the clients are getting what they need.

There's a better approach.

The key to successful financial discussions between clients and agencies is to shift the conversation. Instead of focusing on the tactics delivered for a specific cost, reframe the narrative! Make your proposal...

**A story of the client's and agency's mutual success.**

Here is the process to create a mutual client-agency success story:

1. **Start with the Client's Business Goals and Issues.** Begin by aligning with the client's specific business objectives and challenges. This foundational step ensures

the conversation starts where it should: the business. Clients invest in marketing and agencies to positively impact their business, not for fun. For example, if the client needs to increase awareness by +5% to achieve a sales growth target of +2%, the agency and client can focus on how to meet that awareness goal.

2. **Link Goals to Specific Strategies.** Goals don't achieve themselves — they need actionable strategies. Both parties should agree on the strategies that will drive the desired result. In the example above, the strategy might be a broad reach awareness campaign.

3. **Identify Tactics that Fit the Strategies.** With strategies in place, the agency can recommend tactics that align with the agreed-upon approach. For instance, the tactics might include a brand campaign with TV, video, digital, and social assets.

4. **Define Specific Agency Deliverables.** The agency should outline specific deliverables they'll provide, moving from broad tactics to concrete finished work. In this case, deliverables might include a campaign strategy, creative platform, and assets such as three 30-second videos, three 15-second videos, and weekly paid social posts.

5. **Define the Investment Needed.** With deliverables defined, the agency can share the cost of their contribution to achieving the client's goals. This step is about transparency and aligning expectations.

6. **Recap How the Investment Achieves the Client's Goals.** The final, critical step is to bring the conversation full circle. Recap how the agency's investment and deliverables will help the client achieve their business objectives. This creates a mutual success story where the client achieves their goals, and the agency is fairly compensated for their work.

### Why This Works

This approach fosters budget and scope harmony by focusing on shared success. While it doesn't eliminate the need for competitive pricing or fair compensation, it creates a collaborative framework where both parties understand the value of the investment and the expected outcomes.

By developing a mutual success story together, clients and agencies can build stronger, more productive partnerships.

---

### EXERCISE: MONEY

- How does your agency talk about the money?
- Does your agency provide a spreadsheet or cost details without linking those investments to the necessary business impact that the prospect needs?
- What adjustments can you make to your approach when discussing budgets and financials to improve your chances of success?

# CHAPTER 26
# Meeting Basics

The day of the pitch will undoubtedly be stressful and mentally draining as you focus on the intricacies of the presentation. It's crucial to take moments to ground yourself and your team, ensuring you're as relaxed and focused as possible. Here are a few tips and tools to help you avoid any unexpected hiccups and keep your presentation on the path to success.

## Pitch Page

First, it's a good idea to create a "Pitch Page" that provides a brief overview of the proposal's details. This would include pertinent information, such as:

- Prospect business issues
- Implications of those issues
- Prospect decision maker(s)
- Brief decision maker profile(s)
- What the prospect wants to accomplish in the meeting
- Your agency's solutions, including the applicable process, how the solution ladders to the business issues, relevant stories, and case studies
- Desired next steps

## Presentation Checklist

A checklist will help you remember all the minor details that might get overlooked as you focus on the big picture.

### Room Setup

- ☐ Can you get a layout or photo of the room in advance?
- ☐ Can the seating be arranged to enhance interaction?
- ☐ What built-in capabilities does the room offer (whiteboards, tables, A/V, etc.)
- ☐ Is it possible and practical to have refreshments and snacks available for participants?

### Audio/Visual

- ☐ Do you have the tech details of the available equipment?
- ☐ What audio/video components are needed to use the video capabilities (digital screenshare, teleconference software, HDMI, etc.)?
- ☐ Do you have extra batteries, bulbs, and other potentially necessary backups?
- ☐ Does the room have a presentation screen?
- ☐ Are the electrical outlets conveniently located? Do you need an extension cord?
- ☐ Do you have a backup internet connection?

### Materials

- ☐ Easels and flipcharts?
- ☐ Dry erase markers?
- ☐ Placemats?
- ☐ Leave behinds?

### Look The Part

Confidence and charisma can help make a lasting connection. How you look and represent your agency is just as important as any content you're going to present, if not more so. Your proposal could be brilliant, but if you're a sloppily dressed, mumbling, fidgety presenter, nothing you share will matter because you won't have a captured audience.

Dress a little more formally than your audience to project an image of professionalism. It's easier to dress down by removing a jacket and tie to "roll up your sleeves and dive in" than it is to make jeans and an agency T-shirt impressive in a boardroom.

### Get Comfortable

If possible, arrange for an advanced visit before your presentation so you have a full understanding of the space before you walk in to pitch. Spend some time alone in the presentation room and visualize yourself making the presentation. Practice moving around the room, including entering, standing, walking around the space, sitting, and making introductions.

### Keys to a Confident Presentation

Moving around during your presentation helps keep your audience engaged. At the same time, you want to walk with purpose so you're not pacing back and forth. Keep these things in mind:

- Move intentionally but slowly, stopping to make a point or tell a story.
- When standing still, have your feet about shoulder's width apart.
- Don't lean against the lectern or table.

- Use hand gestures to reinforce important points.
- Face the audience. Don't turn your back and read from the slides.
- Keep your shoulders toward the audience when gesturing toward the screen.
- Establish good eye contact with the individuals in the room.
- Keep your tone conversational, but your energy should be slightly elevated.
- Avoid mumbling or shouting.

# CHAPTER 27
# How to Run a Prospect-Friendly Agency Visit

A client needs a new agency, and after a diligent process, has narrowed the field to a couple of agencies.

The prospect is thrilled — they've done their research and believe they've identified a few promising agencies. Meanwhile, the agencies are equally energized, knowing they're among the final contenders in the competition.

But any agency decision is an important decision, and the prospect has decided to visit the final couple of agencies (good idea!) to see and experience firsthand what the team is like on their own turf and hear them talk about their offerings and what working with them is like.

## Making the Most of the Agency Visit

A site visit can be an important step in evaluating an agency. To make the most of your visit, we recommend that you approach the visit with a limited number of objectives in mind and keep the visit focused on those topics.

Some clients try to cover too much ground or focus on too many minor issues, which, in our experience, can lead to missed opportunities and even less clarity in the process.

We recommend keeping the visit simple.

For agencies, the key is to remember that this is business, but you're also the host. To ensure the visit is productive, focus on the following:

1. **Co-Plan the Agenda:** Start by collaborating with the prospect to create a clear, mutually agreed-upon agenda. This ensures both parties are aligned and gives the agency a chance to address any questions or concerns upfront. A well-planned agenda sets the stage for a successful visit.

2. **Prep on the Prospect's Business:** Clients hire agencies to solve specific business challenges, not to spend money. Research the prospect's industry, competitors, and potential issues they might be facing. Be ready to ask deeper questions and engage meaningfully in their business.

3. **Let Your Team Shine:** Leadership should open and close the visit, expressing how honored the agency would be to work with the prospect. Beyond that, let your team take the lead. Focus the conversation on understanding the prospect's business — this is where talent and chemistry truly shine.

4. **Build Chemistry & Rapport:** The visit is an opportunity to connect on a human level. This is a people business, and it's crucial that both teams feel comfortable working together. Introduce the prospect to your team, share a meal, and let them see the personal side of your agency.

5. **Showcase Your Culture:** The prospect will be observing your team and agency culture. Are your staff collaborative, lively, and business-like? Ensure your team is comfortable being themselves and that the prospect sees the real agency — one that aligns with their needs and values.

6. **Dive into Deeper Discussions:** Use the visit to have meaningful conversations about business, strategy, philosophy, and culture. This is your chance to showcase your agency's capabilities, knowledge, and experience, and demonstrate how you can help the prospect's business thrive.

7. **Be a Thoughtful Host:** Hospitality doesn't mean extravagance — it's about ensuring the prospect is comfortable. Provide seating, writing space, and refreshments. Ask about dietary restrictions, keep coffee and snacks available, and offer a private space for calls or debriefs.

8. **Suggest Clear Next Steps:** Whether it's starting a relationship or providing additional information, define clear next steps. Both sides have a lot at stake, so it's important to outline what each party is responsible for moving forward.

9. **Follow Up Promptly:** Send a heartfelt thank-you and respond quickly with any requested materials. Request a debrief call as the next step to keep the momentum going.

The partnering between a client and an agency is one of the most important decisions in business. A well-executed visit can help both parties size each other up and lay the foundation for a successful collaboration.

And, remember that this is a dating process! Be yourself. And avoid unforced errors that diminish the potential for an engaging and productive session.

What could possibly go wrong? You'd be surprised! It's crucial for agencies to recognize that unforced errors can significantly dampen the enthusiasm of a visiting prospect. Here are some common mistakes that agencies can easily avoid:

1. **Recommending a Bad Hotel.** It might sound trivial, but recommending a subpar hotel can have unintended consequences. If the prospect stays at the agency's suggested hotel and has a poor experience — like a bad night's sleep or uncomfortable accommodations — it

can cast a shadow over the visit before it even begins. While it's not the agency's fault, a negative hotel stay can impact on the prospect's mood and energy. To avoid this, provide a range of hotel options at different price points and let the prospect choose for themselves.

2. **Not Addressing the Entire Requested Agenda.** The prospect is likely visiting for several reasons, such as a final chemistry check, meeting additional team members, or exploring unanswered questions. Agencies must be diligent in ensuring every question or concern is addressed during the visit. Failing to do so can leave the prospect feeling unresolved or undervalued.

3. **Including Too Many Speakers Outside the SOW.** At this stage, the prospect typically wants to meet the core team that will actually be working on their business. Introducing too many speakers who aren't part of the scope can backfire, creating confusion or skepticism about who will truly be involved. Keep the focus on the key players who will drive the work.

4. **Failing to End on Time.** This is a business meeting, and prospects have schedules to adhere to. If the agency doesn't respect the prospect's time before they're hired, it raises doubts about how time will be managed after the partnership begins. Always aim to end on time — or seek explicit clearance if an extension is needed.

We could add a number of other unforced errors, but you probably get the point: the agency is inviting the prospect into their "home," and the key is to avoid any mistakes that can leave the prospect questioning the agency's fit.

# CHAPTER 28
# Follow Up

Don't let your momentum fade after the pitch. A well-executed follow-up strategy is critical for making a lasting impression and increasing your chances of success. Plus, it's the perfect time to debrief with your team and identify areas for improvement. Incorporate these steps into your post-pitch routine for maximum impact.

## Define The Follow-Up (Before You Leave)

Before the pitch concludes, proactively clarify next steps with the prospect. Confirm their decision timeline and any required revisions, implementation details, or other key dates that emerged during the presentation. This sets clear expectations and demonstrates your commitment.

## Post-Meeting Notes: Capture While It's Fresh

Immediately after the pitch, dedicate time to a thorough review. Revisit your notes and the presentation deck, capturing any key insights or action items that may have been missed during the live session. This ensures a comprehensive record of the conversation and allows you to address any outstanding points promptly.

## Send "Thank You" Notes: Craft a Personalized Thank-You Message

For new clients or prospects, the personal touch of a handwritten note or personal email is incredibly impressive. Write one personally to each of the people on the prospect's team who attended the meeting. It's also a nice touch to send one to anyone on the prospect's team who you may not have met at the pitch but who was integral in pulling it together, such as the CMO's assistant, especially if there is a sense that the pitch involved coordinating complicated elements.

Either way, keep these short and sweet, thanking decision-makers for their time and feedback, but without pushing any agency agenda.

**Send a Summary:**
**Reinforce Your Message with a Summary**

Send a clear, concise recap of the meeting, action items, and timelines to decision-makers within 24 hours to keep you top of mind.

**Download with Your Team**

Hold a brief meeting with all of the pitch attendees from your agency and discuss what went right, what went wrong, decision-maker reactions, lessons learned, tips for next time, and action steps. If there are teachable moments, be careful when they are shared. If a one-on-one conversation is more appropriate, don't reprimand someone in front of the entire group. At the same time, be equally careful about praising any one member of the team, unless there is a consensus or an obvious moment when someone knocked it out of the park or saved the day.

**Stay In Touch: Provide Ongoing Value**

Position yourself as a valuable resource by sharing relevant industry trends, helpful articles, or recognizing their success. This demonstrates your continued interest and expertise without being overly persistent. Remember, it's best to avoid directly asking for updates on your pitch.

### Even When You Lose

Losing is hard, but it's unfortunately a reality of life and business.

Rejection is part of the process. You poured your heart and soul into the pitch, presenting with conviction and confidence. It's natural to feel a sense of loss when the outcome isn't what you hoped for. Recognize the effort you invested and allow yourself time to process the disappointment.

It's important, however, to remember that you DID get in the room. You did the work, and you showed up and pitched your butt off. It's possible you will never know what the final deciding factor was in the decision to go with another agency.

Maintain professionalism above all else.

While disappointment is understandable, it's crucial to accept the decision gracefully. Arguing or criticizing the prospect's choice is never advisable. Instead, prioritize maintaining a cordial and respectful relationship. This approach demonstrates maturity and keeps the door open for future collaborations.

Be gracious with the announcement. This will pay dividends down the road.

Nurture your network. Maintain connections with the people you engaged with during the pitch. They might realize the selected agency isn't the right fit, have upcoming projects perfect for your expertise, or even remember your positive interactions when recommending agencies at a new company.

Ask for feedback. Do so in the context of, "We're always looking to improve the way we pitch business and talk to clients. If you have anything you'd like to share that you think we could have done better, it would be really helpful. We see this as a learning exercise." Sometimes the prospect is unable to give such feedback due to company policies but sometimes they do. Either way, the question shows a respectable level of humility, curiosity, and desire to grow as an agency.

Leave them with a favorable impression. No matter how challenging the loss is, always maintain a cool and cordial attitude. Make sure your final interaction reinforces their positive perception of you.

### PROSPECT-FRIENDLY ACTIONS

**Jen Eiselein, former VP, Marketing and Product Development, VTech**

*"I would encourage agencies that don't win to follow up. If an agency that didn't win the pitch is engaging and wants to understand why, that certainly creates an open door for future engagement. The dynamics of things change so much that something that may not have been a fit a year ago could suddenly be a better fit based on the evolving needs of the business."*

# CONCLUSION

**It's Not About You.**

Think back to the Bruce Springsteen and Jimmy Iovine story from the introduction; it illustrates this point perfectly.

Jon Landau looked Jimmy straight in the eye and said:

"You go back there and say to Bruce, 'I'm here to support you. This is not about me, it's about the album.' You do that and you will have a friend for life."

That story underscores the core principles that drive agency success:

**It's Not About You.**

Ego has no place here.

The starting point for every interaction?

**Talk Less and Listen More.**

And then?

**Talk About the Prospect and Not About the Agency.**

And finally...

**Solve the Prospect's Business Issue.**

That's the bottom line.

The agencies that truly thrive prioritize understanding their clients above all else. They are deeply committed to helping their clients achieve their goals, always meeting their needs first.

**Adopt the Prospect-Friendly Pitch.**

Experience the rewards: increased win rates, a more enjoyable pitching process, and a more successful agency overall.

# Appendix 1: Prospect-Friendly Website Evaluation Criteria

| FOCUS AREA | POTENTIAL POINTS | CRITERIA |
|---|---|---|
| **Positioned** | 20 | |
| Clear Frame of Reference | 10 | Clarity in the type of work or kind of agency |
| Differentiated Positioning | 10 | |
| - Agency philosophy | 6 | Defined and demonstrated on homepage, about us, cases, etc. |
| - Strategic process | 3 | Clearly defined, expressed through capabilities, case studies, creative, thought leadership, etc. |
| - Interaction philosophy | 1 | Clearly defined and expressed in "about us," culture, etc. |
| **Functional** | 30 | |
| Navigation | 10 | |
| - Menus | 5 | Easy to find and use |
| - Search functionality | 5 | Robust search function to quickly and easily find content |
| Great Experience | 10 | |
| - User Friendly | 5 | Readable, viewable, and understandable |
| - Video | 3 | Used for emphasis, videos add value, fast load times |
| - Shareable | 2 | Easy to copy and/or share with others |
| Mobile-friendly | 10 | Mobile and cross-device compatible design |

| **Content Rich** | **50** | |
|---|---|---|
| Capabilities | **10** | Clear and concise with confidence-inspiring details |
| Clients/Industries/ Experience | **10** | Current vs. past, sortable by industry, issue, capability, etc. |
| Case Studies & Work Samples | **10** | Includes challenges, analysis & insights, strategy, tactics & results |
| Bios | **6** | Leadership and key team members, experience, and successes |
| News & Awards | **3** | Up-to-date |
| Offices & Contact Information | **5** | Offices & specific contact information — not just a form |
| Thought Leadership | **5** | Relevant knowledge and expertise (could be business challenges, capabilities, industries, processes, etc.) |
| Downloadable Fact Sheet | **1** | Key info like leadership, locations, size, clients, capabilities |
| **Total Points** | **100** | |

# Appendix 2: Prospect-Friendly Written Proposal Outline

### Section 1: The Cover Letter

- Express enthusiasm and appreciation
- Recap the prospect's business issues and implications
- Briefly highlight how your agency has addressed similar issues for clients

### Section 2: Business Issues

- What we've heard from the client
- Identify the issues that need to be solved

### Section 3: Analysis & Strategy

- Agency analysis that adds great value and what it means to the client
- Key learning and opportunities developed from data and research as well as a review of the consumer, competition, and brand
- Key insights identified

### Section 4: Recommended Solutions

- Present the solutions using your strategic process framework
- Explain how it works
- Position your solution relative to the business issues and implications

### Section 5: Case Studies

- Include an overview of the objectives, goals, work, and results
- Present using the agency Philosophy and Strategic Process
- State how the case study is relevant to the prospect's business issue

**Section 6: Relevant Experience**

- We have the right team!
- Bios of key executives AND day-to-day team
- Answer "why is this person on my business" (experience, skill set, other)

**Section 7: Agency Background**

- Agency Philosophy, Process, Interaction Philosophy
- Capabilities (as relevant to the client's issues)
- Related client experience (as relevant to the client's issues)

**Section 8: Next Steps**

- Detailed proposal?
- Office visit?

**Section 9: Appendices**

- Estimate
- SOW
- Staffing plan

# Appendix 3: Business Profile Template

### Company Profile

What they do, industry, history, ownership, etc.

### Culture

Values, philosophies, mission, vision, CSR practices

### Headquarters & Other Locations

Locations and addresses of key company locations, stores, geographic dispersion

### Financials

Public vs. private, income, revenue sources, EBITDA, stock price, investor coverage

### Headcount

Corporate vs. retail, growing/shrinking, U.S. vs. international

### Products & Services

Offerings, product lines, services, add-ons, new products

### Business, Market & Competitive Context

Recent company/brand/product performance, historical campaign learning, market share, competitive environment, industry research and reputation, sales trends/YOY results.

### Audience

Target markets, targets by product line/category, targets relative to competitors, demographics, psychographics.

### Channel Highlights

Retail, distribution, partners, footprint, unique store themes

### Calendar & Seasonality

Retail calendar, sales seasonality, sales dates, holiday impacts

### Online Presence

Website, ecommerce presence, social presence, digital marketing approach

### Marketing and Agency Partners

Agency support, agency tenure, mix of in-house vs. outsourcing

### Media Spend

How much, what media, shifting investments

### Industry & Competition

Industry trends, industry challenges, competitor market share, strengths, and opportunities

### Business Challenges/Opportunities

Describe any business issues the client may be facing (increase market share, defend against competitive launches, etc.)

# Appendix 4: A Sample Pitch Calendar

| TASK | DAY |
|---|---|
| Create pitch timeline | Day 21 |
| Dissect RFP | Day 21 |
| Draft business profile | Day 20 |
| Determine business issues | Day 20 |
| Confirm participation | Day 20 |
| Draft Q&A questions | Day 20 |
| Determine research & analysis objectives (to drive strategy) | Day 19 |
| Q&A (call or written responses) | Day 19 |
| Design look and feel for presentation | Day 17 |
| Case preparation | Day 17 |
| Desk research complete | Day 16 |
| Proprietary research complete | Day 15 |
| Review research | Day 14 |
| Identify strategic insights to guide proposed solutions | Day 14 |
| Draft strategic approach & rationale for solutions | Day 14 |

| | |
|---|---|
| Briefs (creative, media, etc.) prepared | Day 13 |
| Brief teams | Day 13 |
| Draft budget approach | Day 9 |
| Creative, media, etc. round 1 | Day 9 |
| Final budget | Day 9 |
| Creative, media, etc. round 2 | Day 6 |
| Manifesto video | Day 4 |
| Final proposals (creative, media, etc.) | Day 4 |
| Draft deck complete | Day 3 |
| Review draft content & presentation deck | Day 3 |
| Proof & finalize deck | Day 3 |
| Rehearsal | Day 2 |
| Presentation | Day 1 |
| Thank you note | After presentation |

# Appendix 5: How to Work with Search Consultants

Search consultants play an important role in the agency world.

They may only represent about 25% of agency searches but typically manage the biggest searches. They are important gatekeepers.

Given their role, we're often asked how agencies can work more effectively with search consultants. What's the key? The key to working with search consultants is to recognize that we are a "channel", and to follow the 4 Rs.

## The 4 Rs

There are four key strategies to engaging with search consultants:

1. Readiness: Be prepared before you connect
2. Radar: Get on their radar
3. Relationships: Communicate effectively
4. Reviews: Go all in and follow the rules

## Readiness

Our job is not to market your agency. In most cases (which should be all cases!), the consultant works for the client and is their agent. They should represent the best interests of the client and help narrow down from thousands of agencies to the small group best suited to help the client succeed. For agencies, that means: **be ready**.

A "ready" agency:

1. **Is well-positioned:** Have a clear frame of reference (what kind of agency are you) and a compelling position.

One fellow consultant said, *"Be clear in how you're positioned — culture, capability, and competency."*

2. **Has a prospect-friendly website:** Prospect-friendly websites help visitors find the information they need. The frame of reference and positioning are on the homepage. Capabilities are clear. Current and past client experience is highlighted. Case studies and bios are compelling. Key data like headcount is covered.

3. **Has done their homework regarding the search consultants:** We are similar and yet very different at the same time. Do your homework! There are only about 30 U.S.-focused search consultants, and less than 10 of us do most of the searches. It's easy to figure us out. What kinds of clients do they serve in scale or industry or agency type? Do they require or encourage you to pay to be included in their database (do not do this!)? Do they charge you to be in a review (and certainly don't do this!).

   Doing your research in advance of outreach will prepare you well for any interactions you end up having, and you'll make a better first impression. As one search consultant put it: *"Determine if you should be on our radar. We are hired by national brands that are looking for agencies doing world-class work."*

### Radar

Once ready, you need to get on our radar. Clients don't follow the agency industry as closely as agency execs. We do. We stay current because it's our job. The best way to get on search consultants' radars is to ***be unavoidable***. You want the consultant to *have* to take your call.

Here's how:

1. **Awards & Work that Gets Noticed:** Awards are important because clients don't pay attention to the industry until they have to — and then they start searching. You need to be findable. Awards increase the odds that you are found and provide additional third-party credibility.
2. **The Lists:** Most agency niches have lists, like lists of top agencies in a field or city or "best lists."
3. **Press Coverage:** Many clients do not routinely read the "trades," but consultants do. Trade coverage helps your "findability," builds your reputation, and can introduce agencies to the consultants. Consider hiring a PR pro who specializes in agencies.
4. **Content:** Most agency content is not terribly helpful and doesn't advance their reputation. A successful content program highlights the agency's deep expertise and helps the agency stand out.

Get on consultants' radars. ***Be unavoidable.***

### Relationships

How do you create lasting personal relationships? Through communication and trust. How do you create a strong consultant relationship? In the same way, through communication and trust. We're busy. Treat us with the same respect that you expect, and you'll do well. In essence:

- ✓ Respect our time: Share real news with us (big awards, big new clients, key hires) efficiently.
- ✓ Tailor communications: Share your updates in the manner the consultant desires.
- ✓ Be responsive: Respond to us thoroughly and quickly; if we are asking questions, we are on the clock.
- ✓ Be honest and straightforward. Don't oversell.

# Thank *you*!

*It's Not About You* is, in fact, about so many of you. This book is filled with your stories, your insights, and our shared conviction that it deserved to be written. Without your unwavering support, it would never have been finished.

We are grateful for our publisher, Kingbird Press, and for Shadley Grei, whose early guidance during Covid set us on our way. Thanks to Teri Vannoy, whose sharp eye as a proofreader brings every page to life.

There are countless friends and family across the agency community who offered time, ideas, and inspiration — too many to name but, always appreciated. Extra thanks to those who went above and beyond: Linda Kaplan Thaler and Robin Koval, whose leadership at the legendary Kaplan Thaler Group lit our creative spark; Dooley Tombras, who generously shared his family agency's remarkable story; Jeff Goodby, who revisited *Art Serving Capitalism* in a memorable conversation; and Ashley Walters of Curiosity, a thoughtful friend and advisor more times than we can count. We've learned so much from industry leaders like Neil Smith, Rob Davis, Brad Casper, Mark Figliulo, Mark Astone, Jason Parks, Stephen Woessner, Janet Casey and Kamran Asgar, and many more who inspired us with their wisdom and words.

The Agency Management Institute community, led by Drew and Danyel McLellan, has been a second home for more than ten years. Their friendship, guidance, and generosity have been invaluable.

We're fortunate to count Matt Kasindorf and the 4As as long-time friends and collaborators - steadfast advocates for our industry.

The Mercer Island Group team — Lindsay, Barry, Emily and Iris — have shaped this book with their insight and dedication, propelling our collective understanding of agency success.

None of this would make sense without our family, who fill our lives with love (and our table with Friday night dinners for fifteen!). All our love to Lindsay & Barry, Emily & Elan, Sara & Melanie and Ellie, Sadie, Leila, Solomon, Mateo, Finn and Teddy.

With deep appreciation,

*Robin and Steve*

# About the Authors

**Robin** and **Steve Boehler** are Partners at Mercer Island Group (MIG), a leading marketing management consulting firm dedicated to fostering success for both marketers and agencies. As a top 5 agency search consultancy in the U.S., MIG specializes in matching the right clients with the right agencies across all disciplines — including creative, media, web, and PR — while also enhancing client-agency workflow, briefing, and creative evaluation processes.

**Robin** brings a unique and highly sought-after perspective on client-agency effectiveness, honed through hundreds of sessions with executives from a "who's who" of corporations including Starbucks, Brooks Running, Amazon, Ulta Beauty, Discover Financial Services, Hannaford, Holland America Line, Zillow Group, and Elevance Health. She routinely collaborates with CMOs, crafting strategies for significant business challenges and expertly facilitating the crucial "meetings after the meetings" that guide clients to their ideal agency partners. Robin also counsels dozens of agencies annually on growth strategies, with her "Win More Business with Strategy" workshop credited for helping many secure their largest-ever clients. She is a frequent and respected speaker at industry events sponsored by organizations such as the ANA, 4As, Agency Management Institute and others.

**Steve Boehler** is equally at home advising in a marketer's C-Suite or an agency's boardroom. He helps leading and aspiring agencies refine their positioning, execute strategy training, and provide critical pitch and RFP support. For marketers, Steve leads consulting teams on behalf of diverse clients such as Ulta Beauty, Hyatt, Nintendo, Kaiser Permanente, Microsoft, Seabourn, and Stop & Shop. His agency clients include notable names like BarkleyOKRP, Curiosity, Think Shift, and DEPT. Steve founded MIG after a distinguished career that included serving as a division president in a Fortune 100 company at just 32, and a decade in Brand Management at Procter & Gamble, where he led iconic brands like Tide and Pringles.

**Together,** Steve and Robin offer unparalleled insight and expertise, making them invaluable resources for anyone navigating the complex world of marketing and agency partnerships.

www.ingramcontent.com/pod-product-compliance
Lightning Source LLC
Chambersburg PA
CBHW051446050726
47593CB00005B/1942

* 9 7 8 1 9 6 5 6 2 9 0 7 9 *